Wondering Toward Center

MERCER UNIVERSITY PRESS

Endowed by

TOM WATSON BROWN
and
THE WATSON-BROWN FOUNDATION, INC.

Wondering Toward Center

Kathy A. Bradley

To Lindsey—
Pay attention. Share what
you find.
Blessings!
Kathy A. Bradley

MERCER UNIVERSITY PRESS
Macon, Georgia
2016

MUP/ P527

Acknowledgments

Writers are notoriously insecure beings. We do what we do, which is snatch words out of our brains and put them down on paper or a computer screen in some coherent order, not because it is easy but because—it is a trite but factual expression—we have to, and therefore there is always a question as to whether this necessary thing is a thing that should be, can be shared. Those people who manage to convince us that the answer to that question is yes deserve to be publicly acknowledged.

Along with the families that created and reared me, the Bradleys and Andersons, I owe a huge debt of gratitude to the one who adopted me—the Bolin-King-Klein-Moody clan. Every writer should be so lucky.

To my friends (many of whom have nothing in common other than me), one day I really am going to get you all in the same room. Thank you for feeding me, housing me, nagging me, knowing me, loving me, and believing in me beyond all reason.

Sarah Domet, you are a marvel. That's all.

Thank you once again to Marc Jolley and the staff of Mercer University Press. You really have spoiled me.

Kathy A. Bradley
March 2016

…You don't know me yet.
Knowing takes a long, long time.
And time is all we have,
Never traveling in straight lines.
So memorize each turn and twist.
Just be careful as you go,
For if love is a labyrinth
Then my heart is Jericho.

Mary Chapin Carpenter
"Jericho"

Wondering Toward Center

A Brief Account of What Came Before

I.

The Art Building. It had no name aside from that. Unlike the other classroom buildings, clustered together with surnames of long-dead donors etched into their stone facades, the Art Building stood alone, at a distance from everything else, without so much as an identifying sign erected in the patchy grass out front. A concrete block structure that, except for the abstract metal sculptures scattered across its mangy lawn, could have passed for the mechanical or maintenance department, it had absolutely nothing to recommend it. Except what took place inside.

In January term of my freshman year at Wesleyan College, I enrolled in a course titled "Traditional American Quilt-making." I have no recollection of the other offerings and know only that the idea of receiving academic credit for something that felt slightly rebellious and was definitely a little quirky appealed to the child I still was at that point, the child who had followed every rule she had ever been given and even some she hadn't. The child who was just beginning to see over the tops of the fences that had kept her safe and held her in.

The last time I had taken art was in sixth grade. The classes were held in my town's original high school building, which by 1967 was relegated to the storage of cleaning supplies, surplus books, and memories. Pressed for space and pressed not at all by regulations that would surely have found the construction unsafe, twice a week those of us who had chosen art as our elective visited the old building that smelled of wood and damp and, on days we worked with charcoal or pastels, the fixative that brought to mind banana popsicles.

On the third floor were empty rooms that we unsupervised bus-riders explored in the afternoons while waiting for our transportation home, where pigeons flew freely and old newspapers scuttled across the heart pine floors when the wind came keening through the broken windows. It was also where, one Wednesday afternoon, three boys—boys from broken homes and sad families—accidentally left a smoldering cigarette to gorge itself on all that tinder.

My family drove by the conflagration on the way to prayer meeting that night, and my brother and I pressed our faces to the car windows to stare out at a sky filled with smoke and flames the color of rust. The dark silhouettes of fire trucks and firemen were flat and still against the rising blaze. The old place was not worth saving, and their only job was to contain and extinguish the fire. At eleven years old, I did not consider the possible danger to nearby homes or the loss of a historically significant building. All I could think about was my current art project, a mosaic, a cardboard rectangle onto which I had just begun attaching ragged bits of colored glass.

My previous effort, the drawing of a still life, had been completely uninspired. No amount of shading could make my fruit look three-dimensional, particularly when compared to that drawn by our friend Melanie, "the artistic one." But the mosaic was different. It wasn't meant to be an exact representation. Instead, it could be simply suggestive. It could be, in the language of poetry—something at which I had actually demonstrated some acumen—metaphorical. It was quite possible that with the mosaic I could create a real piece of art, a thing of beauty.

The fire, though, which was itself a thing of strange and dangerous beauty, eliminated that possibility. I could almost see the edges of my corrugated canvas turning orange and curling black, the glue melting, and the shards of glass being buried in a pile of soot.

Eight years later I would enroll in Quiltmaking at

Wesleyan. Maybe I was trying to close a loop. Maybe, in making a quilt, I wanted another chance at creating something out of discarded pieces. Maybe, in this choice, I thought I could prove that there was beauty in me.

The Wesleyan dormitories and administration buildings, red brick Georgians adorned with columns, stone arches, and pilasters, were clustered around a fountain-centered courtyard and oak-lined quad. From that idyllic postage-stamp scene, I hiked every morning in January down a hill to the ugliest place on the whole 200 acres. It was the rainiest winter anyone could remember, and the single sidewalk leading from the main road to the front door of the Art Building was constantly flooded. A great many mornings I arrived with my shoes and socks completely soaked and the hems of my jeans caked in mud.

There is no reason I should remember these details so clearly except that they are in such stark contrast to what happened once Tony Rice, whose jeans and flannel shirts were more rumpled than our own, ambled to the front of the classroom of mostly non-art majors and began sharing what he knew.

What he knew, as far as I could tell, was everything there was to know about art. (Or "the visual arts," as I learned to say in deference to the musicians and actors among the faculty and student body.) Any cold or wet or dreariness that could have sneaked through the windowless metal door on our way in was erased by the painting and drawing, printmaking and sculpture, pottery and weaving to which he introduced us, along with his own work of shoe sculptures in large abstract shapes and clear bright colors straight from a Crayola box.

By the end of the term, each of us was to have completed an actual quilt face, but the real intention of the class was to introduce us not just to quiltmaking but to an assortment of traditional American art forms. One morning we discussed face jugs, the primitive pottery made in the mountains of Georgia and North Carolina. Going into the ceramics studio to observe how pottery was made, we clustered around an intense and quiet student who perched at the potter's wheel while Mr. Rice explained the process.

The girl on the stool attached to the wheel sat with her spine straight and tall, like a dancer's. Her slender arms ended in delicate hands that curved around a mass of wet and shiny, slick and slimy clay. Mr. Rice probably explained why she frequently dipped her fingers into the nearby bowl of water, how she knew when to pull up and when to press down on the shapeless gray blob, when the resulting vessel would be ready for the kiln. I'm sure he did, but what I remember very clearly from that demonstration, the one thing that I have carried with me like a small tattoo on my brain, is his explanation of centering.

That a lump of clay, shapeless and heavy, could be thrown onto a spinning disc and not fly off, could find its center of gravity with the assistance of two sensitive and well-trained hands and from that point defy the pull of the spin, could hold its place and yet yield itself to being formed into something useful and beautiful was nothing short of magic.

Over the next three and a half years, as I made good grades and better friends and felt myself moving away from or at least examining the assumptions of my rearing, I often thought of that rainy January morning. Moving through days that were both studio and laboratory, I was beginning to understand, I thought, what it meant to be centered. I was the lump, and under the tutelage of my professors, the influence of my friends, and the unappreciated shelter of Wesleyan itself, I was taking shape, being formed into something useful and sturdy, if not quite beautiful.

I had found myself—a bright but naive, articulate but insecure first-generation college student—on the spinning potter's wheel, oblivious to things like centrifugal force and centripetal acceleration, but quite amazed that I was somehow managing to cling to the slick, flat bat and avoid being flung out into space in bits and pieces.

It did not occur to me that the language itself—being centered—used the passive voice.

II.

From the first time I heard the story of Lot's wife, saw my Sunday school teacher remove the disobedient woman's paper doll representation from the flannelgraph board and replace it with a tall white tower, I have understood the danger of looking back.

I was fifteen when I decided that I would go to law school. Awkward and unsure in social situations as all but the most unusual fifteen-year-olds are, I knew exactly how to please my parents and my teachers and did so with great enthusiasm and without hesitation, an endeavor that should have left little time to dwell on either the awkwardness or the unsureness. Should have, but did not. I was acutely aware in every moment—even on report card day when my stiff progress report contained nothing but A's, even at the spend-the-night parties at my house to which all my friends wanted an invitation, especially on the nights of Homecoming and prom—that I lacked some essential quality that allowed me to fit in.

To the equation was added the era. It was the 1970s. The doors to law school and medical school and dental school, so long narrowed if not completely closed to women, were widening. From every direction, from magazines and television shows and college admissions brochures, I was delicately reminded that doors cracked opened could easily close if women did not take advantage of the opportunities in sufficient numbers. Female applicants to professional schools were, in fact, increasing in number, and they were wearing t-shirts that said things like, "A woman needs a man like a fish needs a bicycle." To someone with a not-yet-fully-developed prefrontal cortex, the bravery and cleverness of such actions were attractive. And, in a paradoxical way, they seemed a safe route away from the awkwardness and unsureness.

What I did not hear was anyone telling me that my love of words, my fascination with story, my fondness for imagination could be turned into anything other than good grades. What was never suggested was that the daydreams of the little girl who learned the word *author* in second grade and decided that one day she would be one had anything to do with that other word, the word that had suddenly gained such societal prominence—*career*. The possibility of a life, a livelihood, based on that which brought me joy and satisfaction as opposed to outside reward, fueled by passion as opposed to the desire to please, resulting in the creation of some shareable thing from the sounds and images that were constantly perambulating through my head seemed never to have occurred to anyone, least of all me.

What I heard was that smart girls, girls like me, had a responsibility to our gender. What I did not hear was any mention of a responsibility to the gifts that lay within me, to the words that sought expression, to myself.

Even at my liberal arts college, where I was surrounded by people who studied and encouraged creativity, who demonstrated it themselves, and who had taken less conventional, even eccentric professional paths, I did not allow myself the gift of reconsideration. Not when my pre-law advisor suggested I fill my elective slots with creative writing courses, not when I became editor of the college magazine, not when I sat in the classrooms of Julia Ketcham and Leah Strong and Arch Beckelheimer and felt as though I had just come home from a long journey through a harsh landscape. The thought of changing my mind never crossed my mind.

And so, I found myself, upon graduation, moving my belongings from my dorm room at Wesleyan into an apartment four and a half miles up Forsyth Road, where its name changes to Vineville Avenue, and walking into the marble-tiled foyer of Mercer Law School, fulfilling the intentions of the tenth grader I hardly remembered, knowing very little beyond the fact that there was no danger of my turning into a pillar of salt.

For the next three years, the hands that cupped my malleable self and kept it centered were the Socratic method and the Uniform System of Citation. At the end of those three years of competitive and often debilitating spinning, a law degree in one hand and a letter from the State Board of Bar Examiners proclaiming that I had passed the Bar in the other, I had done what I had said I was going to do. I accepted the first (and only) job offer I received, and moved back home.

A small-town lawyer serves on boards and committees. A small-town lawyer calls bankers by their first names. A small-town lawyer knows how to get a neighbor's drunk teenager out of jail and then talk football and babies and barbecue while waiting in line at the funeral home to express words of genuine sympathy to the widow of the man who sold her daddy his first tractor, all within a couple of hours. She works hard at being dependable and cheerful and trustworthy, as though there was within her grasp a rank of Girl Scout, complete with badge sash, created just for grown women.

And there were the other things, good things. A nephew and then a niece to watch and teach and love. Friends to tend. A house, Sandhill, to build on the family farm. The vessel I had become turned out to be useful if flexible. One day a wide bowl, the next a slender vase. I had, it appeared, found the center, and I was as complete a piece of pottery as I ever imagined I would be.

III.

The place to which I returned, a farm about eighteen miles from town and the acreage to which my family had moved during my senior year in high school, was not truly home in any way other than the sense of a permanent address. Cousins of various degrees lived nearby, and about two miles away was a weathered tenant house where my father was born, but beyond that I knew virtually nothing about the geography, the topography, or the history of the 450 acres on which I had landed. I had a vague notion of the land lines and could identify only the most ubiquitous of the trees. I had some understanding of the wildlife that shared the acreage but had never met any of them face to face. I returned to the dirt as little more than a reluctant but resigned tourist. And a tourist is what I would remain for some time to come.

Then one fall, one of those boards on which I served went to Highlands in the mountains of North Carolina on a retreat. On Saturday afternoon the board president and hostess for the weekend, Gloria, took some of us on a hike during which she identified every wildflower we encountered and, for most of them, offered additional information with regard to local folklore or medicinal uses. She also named every tree and mountain within view and, at times, sung snatches of an aria or two as an integral part of some story she shared. She moved rapidly and easily between the professorial tones of a botanist and the excited jabber of a toddler. "Look! Look! It's a lady's slipper! Over here! Right there! See? Trillium! And Dutchman's pipe! Come look at this jewelweed! Don't you just love it?"

She displayed not only knowledge but also awe and astonishment, both at nature and at her presence in it. She was not a tourist; she was a participant in the exuberant, elaborate show being put on every day right outside her door. I was embarrassed at my ignorance and envious of her ease in moving through the world of things that lived and died, rose and set.

Before we left Highlands, I marched myself into Cyrano's Bookstore and bought a copy of *The Audubon Society Field Guide to North American Wildflowers*, intent on learning, if nothing else, what to call the purple and white and yellow weeds that grew along the ditches back home.

With that fat little book and a freshly sharpened pencil, I started taking walks, making notes of the dates when I first saw and identified spiderwort, goat's rue, blue curl. The dogs, my Ginny and her sister Fritz, went with me, and before long we had left the rutted and dusty road and ventured out into the woods, following the old timber roads as though they were familiar paths. I found gopher tortoise burrows and the rusted lips of turpentine cups protruding from old pine trees. I learned the run of the branch and the rise of the hill behind the pond. I came home with my hair full of twigs and with cockleburs strung up my pants legs like stars in a new constellation.

The walks turned into wandering. The book and the pencil got left at the house. The voices that never stopped reminding me of chores and expectations got softer and their interruptions less frequent. And yet, for a long time my wandering felt like an intrusion. I was, after all, the prodigal, the one who left for seven years and, even now, left again every morning to return when the day was over. I half expected the fence to deliberately trip me or one of the trees to ask for identification.

I did not yet understand how little space existed between me and the leaves that fell in showers on my shoulders in the last autumn sunshine or the stars that spread in waves across the winter sky. I did not understand it, but I sensed it. Like numbness beginning to thaw, I felt the pinpricks of pain. I rambled with no purpose beyond looking in order to see, listening so that I might see hear.

One of the sounds I heard was that of pottery beginning to crack.

IV.

We were not beach people. My family, that is. The conservative church in which I was reared prohibited "mixed bathing," a rule that resulted not only in separate boy/girl swimming periods at church camp (Though the baptismal service held in the pool at the end of the week involved both genders, each was fully clothed when dunked in the name of the Father, the Son, and the Holy Ghost.), but also in the necessity of declining all invitations to pool parties. It meant no vacations at the beach as well, since mixed bathing was the entire purpose of going to the beach, and even if one did not participate, one could not help but observe. Though we lived less than an hour and a half away from the coast, I was thirteen years old the first time I saw the ocean.

It was on Jekyll Island, and I stood on the long, empty beach while the other members of Girl Scout Troop 370 laughed and splashed and put on Coppertone. I stood and I stared.

I had watched the landscape change as we neared the island in the troop leader's station wagon, seen Spanish moss dangling heavily from live oak limbs as big around as a man's waist, smelled the salt marsh and couldn't decide if it was pleasant or disgusting, but nothing had prepared me for the sudden wideness, the endless flatness, the simultaneously overwhelming and comforting sensation of standing on the seashore.

I had learned to swim in the Ogeechee River, its water brown like strong tea, murky and mysterious. I had spent hours swimming back and forth across the dark-water pond in our backyard. I was not prepared for the gray and silver and blue. I was not prepared for the sound of the waves, even at low tide, slapping in syncopated rhythm at the sand, louder than anything I'd ever heard and yet making me feel as though I need only whisper to join it in conversation. It took my breath.

And it kept it. The ocean held my breath for me until thirty years later when I came back for it.

V.

I was forty when I fell in love. An embarrassingly late age to allow oneself to fall over or through or into anything, especially the uncontrollable state of desiring to be known and believing that perhaps one may have run into the single person out of six billion who is capable of doing that. And an uncomfortably late age at which to consider what exactly one does with that desire and that discovery.

What one does to minimize the embarrassment and maximize the comfort, to maintain the illusion of control, is deny that it has happened. Deny to anyone who asks and even those who don't, deny to anyone who might suspect and especially to yourself that this one out of six billion is different from any other one. Deny that the world has changed, that the sunset is more miraculous and the moonrise more magical, that there are more stories to tell than there ever were before. And, whatever else one does, one must deny the feeling of slipping, ever so slowly, from the grip of the potter's wheel.

In the years since my first sight of the ocean, I had visited the beach only occasionally and thought of it rarely. The souvenir recollection of that first encounter, sealed away in a vault in my memory, was too fine, too valuable to be pulled out for everyday use. Sometimes, when I read a book set at the seashore or heard someone talk about a weekend at the beach, the memory surfaced involuntarily and I felt an improbable recognition. But those moments were rare. I never suspected that the sound in my ear that would not go away was the ocean.

The vault finally opened when I followed the one in six billion to St. Simons Island. Separated from the mainland by four miles of causeway that cross a salt marsh and five tidal rivers, St. Simons is a barrier island. It protects the Georgia coastline from the ravages of the Atlantic Ocean. There is little that protects the island itself.

On weekends and the occasional day trip, we wandered down East Beach and up Gould's Inlet as I had wandered in the woods and across the fields. I collected shells and driftwood and stories. I grew accustomed to being unable to tame my hair. I laughed at myself becoming territorial with tourists.

I sat on the beach for hours watching the one windsurf, growing smaller and smaller as the sail filled, bending first one way and then the other to stay upright. I forced myself into stillness when he became invisible, when fear rose without permission into my throat and lodged there, until eventually he reappeared on the horizon, a dark spindle against the blue sky, making his way back.

Once, at 3 a.m., we went walking along the edge of the water where the low tide made soft foam and the breaking waves out past the sandbar sounded like thunder. Trails of luminescent colors exploded in the water where our feet moved. Cobalt blue, chartreuse, the whitest white I'd ever seen. We walked in circles, dragged our hands in curves and curls, and with every movement the colors flashed and flamed. The only thing that could draw our attention away from the fireworks display at our feet was the sudden appearance of a shooting star.

We walked all the way from Gould's Inlet to the Coast Guard Station. We climbed up into the tall red lifeguard's chair. The horizon that seemed so distant in noon's brightness felt no more than an arm's length away in the moonlight.

It was in those moments, those sometimes still but never silent moments, that I learned to hear in the call of the ocean, to recognize in the roar of the surf, the tuning fork to which I could and would turn in the moments of life's dissonance. I realized that just as the farm and Sandhill were mine, so was this place. I held not one square inch of it in fee simple, but every last acre in my heart.

I realized, too, that I had reclaimed the breath the ocean had taken so many years before, and I was slowly slowly slowly letting it go.

VI.

In the ocean, I found the other half to the set of bookends for which I had been searching, the sturdy steady supports that would hold the words together, keep their spines upright, make their names readable. The land on one end reminded me from whence I had come, and the sea on the other beckoned me to exploration of where I'd never been. Between the bookends I found a home.

The land and sea became my classroom and my church, the places to take my deepest wonderings. Scrub oaks and sea oats, wild turkeys and sandpipers whispered, sometimes shouted, questions and answers. Moons rose and suns set, posing riddles. Streams laughed and waves danced and fields brandished swords, all beaten into the ploughshares of parable. I learned to see with greater clarity and breadth, to recognize patterns, to rest in the consistency of cycles. I felt my own heartbeat slow to the rhythm of these places I loved.

I had been seduced by the speeding drone of the potter's wheel into the idea that being centered, balanced, and well behaved was the best I could do or be, and the seduction had lasted for years. One of the results of the *ritardando* was that the wheel, too, began to slow and the force that held me to it weakened. The feelings of responsibility that made me see myself as the fulcrum on an antique balance scale lost their charm and I came to my senses, quite literally. I tasted an acorn, smelled the damp earth of a marsh hammock, listened to a buck snuffle and blow mere yards from the cold puffs of my own breath. I scratched my fingers on barnacles and barn wood. I stared with incredulity at all I had been missing, all I had ignored, and, with the fervor of the newly converted, felt compelled to share.

So I wrote.

When I began writing the newspaper column in 1996, it had been years since anything other than a demand letter or brief or motion for summary judgment had found its way to paper through my hands, years since I'd scribbled in a journal or played with a poem, so I approached the task every other week with some ambivalence. I was happy to have a justifiable reason to write (I promised I would. I have a deadline. The editor expects it.), but I did not trust myself to write anything worth reading. I borrowed heavily from the stories told to me by other people, particularly my family, and included a substantial amount of humor. I made it easy for the newspaper readers, my people, to read and reward me at church or in the drug store with, "I enjoyed Sunday's article." And that was enough. For a while.

What I eventually realized was that the exile in which I had been living, the separation from writing, was self-imposed, that no one was denying me the comfort and safety of my truest home, the place where words are strung together like the tiny letter beads on newborn hospital bracelets…no one except me. No one had ever said, "You are prohibited from writing." How and, more important, why I did it for so long, inflicting upon myself a sort of anorexia of expression, remains the kind of mystery for which there is no solution, only the occasional weary sigh.

It was the wandering, the discovery of the wideness and wildness of the world that lay at my feet, the exploration of the sounds and smells and the craving to share what I had found that finally made me hungry. It forced me back to the table where the words waited, where the stories lay napping. There was, I discovered, only one way to answer any of the questions, to understand any of the mysteries, to address the wondering: to tell about it.

And I could not tell about it if I thought that the center of anything could be found within myself.

The potter's wheel had finally stopped. The metaphor upon which I had lived my entire adult life was broken.

VII.

I don't remember exactly when I started collecting stones.

Someone I knew went to Europe and brought me back a smooth, flat one from the shore of the North Sea. The size of a silver dollar, it was dark gray and had a single pale striation running through it. It reminded me of a pin-striped suit, smart and trim with the cold of the sea inside, and when I held it between my palms it took a long time for the warmth of the blood pulsing through my hands to chase away that cold.

I started paying more attention to stones after that, and, as though beckoned, they began appearing in my hands, gifts from other people on other travels who somehow knew, without being specifically told, that I needed stones. Stones from other seashores, stones from mountain paths, even stones from parking lots. I would sit sometimes at the window, looking out over the fields at the moon rising, and rub the stones between my fingers as though they were pages of Braille.

Late one winter, walking in an unfamiliar wood, I watched the sun grapple its way through a thicket of bare branches, pear-colored pools of light collecting on fallen leaves. The vague path that wound among the trees was strewn with the occasional empty can, evidence that others had been there not so long before. We, the one and I, moved slowly. Our feet made a rustling sound as we stepped through the leaves. An occasional twig broke beneath the weight of one of our shoes and, in the cool air, the snap was sharp and loud.

The talking was soft and low. Less conversation than confession. I listened more than I spoke. Nearing the edge of the wood I knew I was nearing a choice. There were two possible options, and with either one everything would change.

I reached down and picked up a large stone, a rock. It weighed probably five pounds. It was rough and oddly shaped. "I want this rock," I said. I decided to take it home. I wrote on the bottom the location from which it had come and the date on which I had found it, the date I walked in an unfamiliar wood and heard a story and made a choice.

I placed it in a flowerbed. A temporary location. It would stay there until I gathered enough stones, enough significant stones, to build myself a labyrinth, an idea that had appeared like the skywriting of some barnstorming daemon across my brain.

I didn't know much about labyrinths at the time. I'd seen photos of the one at Chartres in my French textbooks; I knew the story of Theseus and the Minotaur; and I knew that in recent years there had been a renewed interest in them, particularly among people who called themselves "spiritual, but not religious." I had not, however, actually seen or walked a labyrinth, a fact that did not prevent me from surveying from the kitchen window the perfect spot at Sandhill on which to lay one out.

I managed to collect a few stones—one from a national seashore without realizing I was breaking the law when I did it and one from a beautiful glen in the North Carolina mountains, along with that first one from the woods of golden sunshine where the choice I made turned out to be the wrong one. On each stone I wrote with my big black Sharpie its provenance and the date when I found it. I was going to build labyrinth of significant moments.

That was the plan.

A lot happened over the next five years. I wrote a book. I finally used my passport. I welcomed a new generation to my family and buried two people whose absence still leaves me stunned and immobile at times. I didn't build the labyrinth. The one in the side yard. The one made of footnoted stones. Skywriting fades and worthy building blocks are rare.

VIII.

For most of my life I envisioned time as linear. I blame this perception only a little on the fact that I never took physics and mostly on the timelines that showed up along the bottom edges of every social studies book I was ever issued. The arrows pointed in only one direction and straight ahead. Occasionally there would be parallel timelines on the same page, but they never touched, never intersected. The impression was that each of the lives and civilizations represented was completely contained—neither impacting nor impacted by any other—between the black dot on the far left margin marking the beginning and the corresponding dot on the far right margin marking the end.

I gradually came to recognize the flaw in that idea, an acknowledgment that resulted, in large part, from the task of writing a newspaper column, twenty-five column inches every other Sunday. I began without parameters, just the request to "write something" as often as I liked, and that lack of constraint has remained for the fifteen years that I have maintained the discipline.

Fifteen years. That's fifteen Advents and fifteen Lents,

fifteen trudges through Ordinary Time. Fifteen winters, springs, summers, and autumns. Fifteen times of writing through the turning of the calendar, telling the stories that have come to me without being summoned, stories that led me to the undeniable conclusion that time is not a single straight line. It is a spiral.

A spiral in which, on which, with which I have been moving, coming back again and again to the same points in space—the same people and places and lessons—over and over. A single spiral of dawn to noon to dusk to night and back to dawn. A single spiral of planting followed by weeding followed by harvesting followed by lying fallow in preparation for planting again. A single spiral of birth then growth then decline then death then...something.

A spiral in which, on which, with which every created thing held, holds, will forever hold a spot.

Without a course in physics, without a single lecture on fractals, simply by paying attention to the stories, I have learned to see all that has ever existed in a fallen pine tree, to hear all that is in the call of a bobwhite quail, to know all that will ever be in the rising of a full moon over a cotton field. I can balance on the edge of the ocean and taste the cosmos, watch a storm cloud swallow a lake and smell forever.

The farm has been my teacher. The ocean my tutor. Every cell of creation my Annie Sullivan, demanding my attention, grasping my hands, spelling out in a language I did not know the single mystery: We are all connected, to the earth and to each other, and it is our stories that keep that connection alive.

It takes faith to write the words you know are true, words you are certain that you mean, even when you have to admit that you do not know exactly what they mean, let alone whether they are literally true.

Kathleen Norris, *Amazing Grace*

January 16, 2011

There's a church in Grand Rapids, Michigan, that used to be a shopping mall. I've never seen it, but I can imagine that its architecture isn't exactly what one would call traditional. I understand, in fact, that the sanctuary—which they may not even call the sanctuary—is sort of, well, round. Not semicircular with two or three aisles leading up to the pulpit like sun rays on an elementary school bulletin board, but round with chairs or pews placed all the way around the platform where the pastor stands. Interesting.

As I said, I've never seen this church, but I know a good bit about it because I subscribe to its podcast and listen to its pastors' sermons on my iPod while running on the treadmill. I was listening just last week, in fact, when I realized that I'd downloaded not just an ordinary Sunday morning sermon, but the Christmas Eve sermon. I knew this because the pastor started by addressing the parents in the congregation who were obviously concerned about having their little ones in "big church."

"Don't worry," he told them in his soothing voice, "if they've run off. We built this place in a circle for just that reason: eventually they will make it back around."

There was laughter, some of it forced, some of it relieved.

"And when they do make it back around," he continued, "they will be tired."

I cannot say that I remember anything he said for the next couple of minutes. I cannot say that I remember picking up my feet and continuing to run on the treadmill, though I am sure I did because I did not fall. All I can remember is the feeling of being hit in the chest by a wave I didn't see coming, the realization of having heard something of the most profound importance.

I could imagine those children—dressed in warm

Christmas outfits mailed to Michigan by their grandparents, cheeks the color of camellias, smiles open and breathy. They were laughing at the sheer joy of movement, pumping their chubby arms and looking around to make sure that everyone else was running, too.

Running is such a natural thing. We learn to crawl. We learn to walk. We learn to run. We learn that running is faster than walking. We learn that the best method for getting away from something we want to avoid is running.

What too many of us don't learn is that life, like the church in Michigan, is built in a circle. We can run—from decision, from responsibility, from fear or pain—but eventually we will make it back around. No matter how many times we circle the loop, no matter how fast or slow we run, no matter how many water stops we make along the way, eventually (Two days? A month? A year? Ten years?) we will be back where we started and come face to face with that from which we ran.

And we are going to be tired.

Which could be a bit disconcerting given the fact that the decision/responsibility/fear has been sitting there waiting all this time.

Except for one thing: We're all children. Every last one of us. And we know what to do when we're tired. We know where to go when every last dream has died and every last ounce of hope has leached away. We know where to find arms big enough to hold us and all our fatigue and failures. And we know that it is in quietness and trust that we will regain our strength, the strength to stop running.

Sometime into the Christmas Eve sermon, sometime into my run, I noticed that the background rumble had hushed and I could picture the children again, this time curled into the laps of their parents, eyelids flickering, chests rising and falling, each and every one of them having made it back around.

January 30, 2011

Scene One: Ice hung off the eaves of the carport like jagged dragon teeth in a preschooler's drawing of scary. Stiff and unresponsive to the wind that came rushing across the field and crying like a banshee, the ice-covered limbs of the sycamore tree could have been the dragon's claws, sharp and pointed and crooked at awkward angles. Standing in the doorway, huddled inside my overcoat, I would have welcomed a quick puff of the dragon's fire breath—just enough to break the chill until I could get into the car.

I nearly slipped going down the steps, muttered something unintelligible even to myself. I cranked the car, turned on the wipers, and discovered that what I thought was water on the windshield was, in fact, ice. I turned on the defroster and waited. The glass got warmer; I didn't. I tucked my gloved hands into my armpits. It didn't help.

Once on the road, the tires crunched the ice and the frozen ground. The car seemed to move forward without traction, like a train skidding smoothly down a rail. The scenery was all white. I was in a lace bubble.

That was two weeks ago.

Scene Two: The deck was still wet with two days' rain and the ground was soggy and slick. The wind whipped around like a lariat in the hands of a rodeo cowboy and the sycamore tree limbs jerked back and forth in a St. Vitas dance of erratic jolts and twitches. Strands of hair got caught in the free-for-all, snagged in my eyelashes, nearly inhaled as I gasped at the gust of wind that rushed under the carport just as I opened the door.

When I turned on the windshield wipers, they swiped easily across the cellophane-thin layer of water, leaving the glass completely clear but for the thin squiggles sliding down the far sides like red wigglers out of a bait bucket. The road was muddy; the tires sank in the ooze of ruts already eight or ten inches deep. It made me think of the valley a four-year-old's finger makes in still-warm cake icing.

That was this morning.

Winter. Not my favorite season. It is cold and dark. It is claustrophobic. It is too long. But it has its moments.

Like last Sunday afternoon. I could stand the incarceration no longer and went to get the dogs. They were as eager to get outside as I was, and the three of us set out like kids at recess, eager and breathless. The breeze was a tad cool, but gentle, licking at my face and their fur. The few bird calls we heard came darting through the crisp air in irregular rhythms, and the winter light, that angled laser that can transform frost directly into mist without becoming water, was so sharp that it made everything in the landscape look as though it were drawn by a pin-prick sharp No. 2 pencil.

I found a dead bird in the middle of the road and stopped to be amazed at the infinitesimal number of feathers, each one shaded in three different colors, that came together to make three broad horizontal bands. I found a scrub oak, no more than three feet high, growing in the sandy ditch and sprouting tiny acorns the size of a thimble. The dogs found an armadillo to chase into the branch, only to lose it as it burrowed into a perfectly round hole, and still came away with their tongues wagging in that gleeful, generous dog way.

It is four miles to the highway and back. (The dogs don't go quite that far; they stop when they get in sight of the asphalt—something telling them that they don't belong there—and wait for me to circle around.) It is a good distance for walking and, on this day, for finding things. I found beauty in death and promise in smallness. The dogs found joy in the unattainable. And we all found a vision of winter that was something more than cold.

Winter. Not my favorite season. But, like everything, it has its moments.

February 13, 2011

Making soup is therapeutic.

First, you gather the vegetables: potatoes dense and slightly rough, carrots gnarled and wrinkled, celery stringy and still carrying dirt in its pockets, and onion slick beneath its papery skin. You peel the potatoes and carrots, watching brown and orange curls of skin fall into the sink beneath the long strokes of the vegetable peeler. They pile onto each other like children wallowing in autumn leaves.

Then you chop. Cubes of potato and onion, discs of carrots, demilunes of celery. The solid sound of metal moving through organic matter. Chop. Chop. Chop. The knife gets stuck in the potato every now and then, its starch making glue on the blade. You stop, wipe it off, and begin again. It moves through the celery with the rapidity of a sewing machine making a long seam. Little mountains grow on the cutting board, little mountains of effort.

Next you take a heavy pot, one that requires two hands to lift, one that reminds you how strong you are. You fill it about a third of the way full, maybe with water, maybe with broth or stock. You scoop up the vegetables with your hands and drop them into the pot, smiling with each satisfying splash. They slide into the liquid and into each other. They look like jewels.

You might add salt and pepper at this point. Maybe bay leaves. It's your soup. Season to taste.

You turn on the heat—medium low at this point—cover the pot, and leave it for a while. Fifteen minutes. Maybe twenty. Maybe thirty. Just depends on how long it takes for the vegetables to become tender but still crisp.

While you wait you clean up the mess.

Once the vegetables are ready, you decide what kind of soup it will be. Does it want tomatoes? Does it want chicken and noodles? Does it want beans? Does it want the leftover corn and green beans in the Tupperware container that falls out of the refrigerator every time you open it?

Put it in, turn up the heat, cook a little longer. However long it takes. This is soup. It isn't soufflé.

When it's ready, you get a bowl, a big bowl, and fill it up. You watch the steam rise in silver wisps. You resist the almost irresistible urge to taste it right away. You will burn your tongue. You know you will.

You lean down to smell it, to feel the steam hit your cheeks. You put your hands around the bowl. It is too hot to hold. You remember reading that the reason Japanese teacups have no handles is that the Japanese know that if the cup is too hot to hold the tea is too hot to drink.

You distract yourself by finding a spoon, a napkin, maybe some crackers or a corn muffin, something to soak up what will be left at the bottom and unreachable by the spoon.

Finally, just at the moment when you are sure you are going to die from anticipation, you venture a tiny sip from the edge of the spoon and, yes, yes, the soup is cool enough to eat. To eat, to slurp (if you are alone), to be drawn not just into your mouth and belly but also into your very veins, easing away more than hunger—anger and loneliness and frustration and fatigue.

Ah, soup.

Making soup is therapeutic. Because it's a lot like making life.

You gather the makings and trim them to fit your pot. You turn up the heat. You throw in a few surprises at the last minute. You wait while all the flavors meld. And then you fill yourself with it, with all of it.

And you remember—please, please remember—that it's your soup, your life. There is no recipe. Only the matter of figuring out what you crave.

February 27, 2011

It is not spring. One look at the calendar confirms it, but on this Saturday morning you could fool anybody. The branch is ringing with overlapping bird calls and the sky is baby blanket blue. The breeze is so slight as to not seem a breeze at all, but something like the close breath of a lover. There is no resisting the pull.

In shorts and a t-shirt I take a book outside to the deck and start to read. And in less than ten minutes I start to wheeze.

I am allergic to the ligustrum bush that grows at the corner of the house just off the edge of the deck. Eight or nine feet tall, its thick leaves stay beautifully green all year and it requires no attention except the occasional pruning to keep it from completely obscuring the bedroom window nearby. Said beauty and self-sufficiency are what have kept it alive for the ever-how-many years it's been since I discovered that its pollen, inhaled into my respiratory system, result, in a significant decrease in breathing function.

What I always do, in response to the ligustrum's attack, is sigh, gather my things, and go inside. Without thinking.

But today—what is it about today?—I don't. Today I sigh, gather my things, go inside, and make a decision. Today is the last day that I will be hindered, hampered, prevented, precluded. Today is the day I act.

Mama and Daddy are outside, too, duct-taping hose pipes together to irrigate some newly planted grape vines. I walk down to their house, cross the yard, and make my request: I ask Daddy, sometime when he has time, not necessarily today, just sometime, to take his chain saw (It's a big bush.) to my house and cut down the ligustrum bush.

"What about now?" he asks, just as I knew he would. "But I'll tell you this. If you just cut it down, come spring it's going to sprout back up. Why don't we pull it up with the tractor?"

And so it is that the John Deere 7810, with the harrow still attached and a chain with links as big as ham hocks attached to that, rumbles into the yard at Sandhill to pull up a bush. It takes less than three minutes. Total.

And how many years have I wheezed and sighed?

Later, when the blue in the sky has faded to chambray and the shadows are falling from the west, I go back outside with my book and start to read. And continue reading. No wheezing. I take a deep breath. Another one.

How lovely to sit in the sunlight, feel the live stillness of the afternoon, absorb the silent tension of the earth about to be awakened.

I close my book and consider the lesson of the ligustrum. Are there other things that need to be pulled up? Not pruned, not trimmed back, not cut down to sprout again, but pulled completely out of the ground and dragged away to die. I wonder what attitudes or expectations have been cutting off my breath for years, what postures I've taken or defenses I've maintained in fruitless attempts to catch my breath, what fears have kept me from exhaling.

I am reminded that the Hebrew Bible uses the same word ("ruach") for both breath and spirit. What have the ligustrums of doubt and anxiety done to my spirit? What have I missed? What have I lost? Why was it so easy to just get up and go inside?

For a moment I feel smothered with regret, suffocated by anger at myself and my failure. Forgive me, Father, for I have sinned.

Something draws my attention to the spot where the ligustrum used to be. Its roots were wide but not deep. The ground is barely disturbed, turned up just enough to welcome my trowel and some new growing thing.

I raise my gaze from the hole and realize how different the view is now. The horizon has opened. I can see the road.

I close my eyes, lift my chest, expand my lungs. And, in

the calm, I feel my breath, my spirit rise.

March 12, 2011

It is grainy and gray, faded and fragile to the touch, a newspaper clipping from 1966. I am bent over it with a combination of amusement and incredulity. The caption says that it is a photograph of Girl Scout Troop 370 on a field trip to the Statesboro *Herald*. It identifies the twenty or so girls, row by row. There in the middle is my name.

I don't remember the visit to the newspaper. I don't remember Mr. Coleman showing us the printing press. I recognize very view of the faces in the photo. That is what creates the sense of incredulity. The amusement arises from the smile—the goofy, tight-lipped grin—on the face of the little girl that was Kathy Bradley. I can't help laughing out loud.

And I can't help staring.

Ten years old. Fifth grade. Mrs. Trapnell's class at Mattie Lively. That was the year my friend Gail got rheumatic fever, the year I got so good playing marbles with the boys at recess, the year I got my long ponytail cut. It was the year I went to Mrs. Russell's classroom for reading, was the narrator of the end-of-school program, and spent a week in June at Camp Safety Patrol.

I remember all that, but I don't remember this imp, this scamp, this child named Kathy who might just burst at any moment from the sheer volume of joy that has risen up through her chest and into her face. What has made her so cheerful? Is it the jaunty green felt beret? Is it the excitement of the field trip? Or is it just being ten years old?

"The great thing about getting older," Madeleine L'Engle, the writer best known for her children's fantasy books, once told the *New York Times*, "is that you don't lose all the other ages you've been." The quote comes to mind later as I find myself contemplating the little girl with the silly smile. If

I have not lost her, where is she?

Certainly she remains in my still-strong penchant for the cookies she sold, but I am not certain that I can detect her features in the face I see in the mirror each morning. I cannot swear that her curiosity or self-confidence or insouciance lingers in the posture I feel compelled to maintain most days. And I am absolutely sure she is not racing me to bed on the nights when life's inevitable blows leave me spent in body and spirit.

It is not so many days later when I see a couple of Girl Scouts camped out at a grocery store entrance, card table covered in cookie pyramids of Thin Mints, Trefoils, Tagalongs, and Samoas. I watch from a distance, listen to their sing-song voices call out, "Would you like to buy some Girl Scout cookies?" I am stopped cold.

The words, the timbre, the chill in the air become the shaped notes of a song I know by heart, its sheet music locked in a bottom drawer of my memory. Right then, right there, the ten-year-old me shows up from wherever she'd been hiding, vacationing, held ransom.

She drops a cool, slick marble in my hand and my thumb bends to shoot it. She hands me a Blue Horse notebook and I spread the pages open across its spiral wire to see fat, loopy cursive vocabulary words. She offers me a pair of stark white Keds with a blue rubber label on the heel and I tighten the laces to go outside and play dodge ball.

I look down to straighten my badge sash, and when I look back up she is gone. Except that she isn't. She is exactly where she has always been. With me. Inside me. Me.

March 27, 2011

Two weeks ago one of the young sawtooth oaks in the backyard was still clinging to its winter leaves—tight little wrapping paper tubes of brittle brown. The bigger leaves were long gone; these were the recalcitrant ones, the obstreperous children determined to have their own way.

The air was warm that morning. The sun was bright. The verbena I'd planted last summer at the corner of the deck was already blooming purple and spilling over the concrete edgers I'd put in place to keep it contained. Why was the oak tree still holding on to winter?

I started wondering how, exactly, the tree's new buds might force the leaves to fall, how the sap might begin pumping in a rhythm akin to a heartbeat, each pump jarring the leaf a little looser until eventually, like the criminal hanging by his fingertips from the thirty-story ledge, there is nothing to do but drop. I could almost see the sticky life-juice pushing through the thin bark, could almost hear it screeching with false bravado, "Hey, you! Yeah, you—yesterday's news! Outta here!"

A couple of days later I pulled into the driveway (in daylight, thanks to the time change) and saw the oak tree covered, ballooned in Coke-bottle green buds and matching leaves. The armature of branches was all but completely hidden by the froth. Not a single brown cylinder remained. Not even on the ground.

I've grown accustomed to the natural world's presti-digitation. We cannot watch it closely enough to observe the change as it happens. Nature performs its magic in secret, under cover of darkness or solitude. Overnight the grass needs cutting. In the afternoon you water a rosebud; in the morning it is in full flower; by evening it is fading.

But this was different. Not the ordinary wizardry of spring. That many leaves do not drop and disappear so quickly.

Still studying the suddenly voluptuous tree over my shoulder, I started toward the back steps and noticed the pine cone seeds. They fanned out over the carport floor like fairy dust, salmon-pink translucent wings weighted down by seeds the color of doe eyes. They'd been lifted from their trees of origin, carried across the landscape between earth and sky, and deposited at my doorstep by invisible gusts of warm spring wind.

And, of course, that is how the oak tree got naked so quickly, too. The wind. Warm spring wind.

The new buds chafed for the dead leaves to fall of their own accord and the dead leaves held to the branch with righteous anger. The new buds, full of new life, impatient to see sunlight, feel raindrops, convert carbon dioxide into oxygen, trembled with anticipation while the dead leaves trembled with fear. Neither could do anything but wait.

Wait for the wind. Wait for the outside force. Wait for the shaking that would strip to naked the strong skeleton and re-dress it in newer, better attire.

We all like to think that we are the managers of our lives, that we make the choices and create the timelines, that the decisions of when or if to hang on or let go are ours and ours alone. To take that approach occasionally may be appropriate, but to live one's entire life that way is to live in denial.

We are all trees. We sprout leaves. We produce fruit. We offer shade. In season. But seasons change. And so we must stand in the wind, roots holding us up straight and tall, and watch as it blows and gusts and tears away all that is dead in order that we may see all that is alive.

April 10, 2011

The wildfire had been burning for over a week. I expected to see evidence of it as I passed the green metal road sign that marked the Long County line and drove on down the highway lined with pine trees and wiregrass, but I didn't.

There were no fields black with soot and stubbled with brittle stems and shoots. There were no rapidly dug trenches across the dirt roads that splayed out from the highway like arteries. There were no collapsed barns or tenant houses, defenseless tinder for unhindered flames. The bright white clapboard of Jones Creek Church still reflected the late afternoon sunlight directly into my eyes as I came around the curve, and the marquee at the elementary school announced spring break next week. There was absolutely nothing to indicate that over 4,000 acres had burned.

Nothing except the smell.

And I didn't notice that at first. The car windows were up and it seeped in slowly, a smell something like fresh creamed corn left on the stove unattended and scorched, stuck to the bottom of your best pot in a thick layer of crud that will have to soak overnight before it even thinks of coming loose. Or like your daddy's white dress shirt pressed by a too-hot iron and tattooed with a caramel-colored arrowhead the size of a fist smack-dab on the front pocket. Like that—bitter and sweet at the same time.

I was on my way to the beach—that place of endless sky, endless water, endless sight—so the land's trauma did not stay with me long. I can't help it; it is as though the core of my heart is made of iron, and the closer I get the stronger is the pull so that by the time I reach the highest point on the causeway bridge I am falling like a ball bearing.

I had no plans other than to talk to and spend time with my friends, but Providence had an invitation and a perfect wind, and before I knew it, I was on a sailboat the next day, slicing through the sound like a knife through butter. To the north we could just make out a handful of people riding horses on Jekyll, and just off the port side was the lighthouse at St. Simons and a nearly empty beach. The sails snapped like laundry hung out to dry and the conversation wound in and out of the rigging like children around a Maypole. You could not have asked for a more idyllic setting.

Driving home later, I didn't notice, didn't notice not noticing the smell of burned landscape. Only later did I realize it. It had been twenty-four hours, of course, and perhaps there had been a rain shower to settle the scent or maybe it was just the normal dissipation of chemicals, but that's not what I think.

What I think is that the smell of scorched corn and burned fabric was still wafting over Long County in waves like the ones that follow Pepé Le Pew in the Looney Tunes cartoons and I—or, rather, my brain's limbic system—had chosen not to smell it, had chosen rather to concentrate on the scent of ocean and sunscreen and that peculiar combination of pimento cheese grits and pork barbecue that had been the lunch special at Southern Soul.

Our brains create such interesting scrapbooks. They clip and save the oddest things—one line from the lyrics of a song heard on the radio driving down the highway during a rainstorm, the color of a shirt hanging over the railing on a hotel balcony, the satin smoothness of a scar, the smell of 4,000 acres charred to jagged nothingness. And they organize those things no better than we organize the photographs and programs and movie ticket stubs we are so intent on saving. Some get attached to archival pages with archival glue, labeled with archival ink, but most of them get thrown into a shoebox or shopping bag with a half-hearted promise of return. Someday.

I hold in my hands the reflection of sunlight on water, the laughter of children, the saltiness of my own lips. They are piled in a generous heap and beneath them lies the scent of ash.

April 24, 2011

The sky last night was a bolt of dark-wash denim, the selvage hugging one horizon, the fold the other. And the stars—oh, so many stars—did not twinkle so much as glow, did not shine so much as radiate, radiate like ice crystals with a kind of negative energy. I lay on my back on the deck, the boards like extra ribs pushing into me at regular intervals, and stared up into the darkness interrupted only occasionally by airplanes so small they could have been fireflies.

The Big Dipper was upside down, emptied of whatever it had held, and I felt the same way. The past few days had moved too fast, required too much, offered too little. The sounds of strident voices ricocheted through my head, and the weight of impatience, uncertainty, and misunderstanding shortened my breath. My eyes were constantly darting, never lighting, avoiding concentration. My heart had been rubbed sandpaper raw.

I know what to do when that happens—get very still and listen—and that's what I was doing. At least trying to do.

In the branch the frogs' voices sounded like an old screen door incessantly opening and closing, the rusty springs stretching and contracting in uneven cadence. Somewhere nearby a small animal moved in the brittle brush left where Daddy had burned off the edges of the field. The petunias hanging from the shepherd's crooks swayed pendulously in the breeze, their flimsy petals fluttering in the moonlight like a coquette's eyelashes.

I forced my breaths to grow longer, deeper. I stared at the sky trying to make out constellations, wondered about the people who first saw the pictures, named them, made up their stories. And as I wondered, my thoughts wandered back a few days to a scene I'd meant to remember and had almost forgotten.

I'd been to town to pick up a few things for the yard—something to fill in the hole in the perennial bed, a basil plant (in anticipation of tomatoes), three azaleas for the spot in front of the chimney. The garden center was a busy place that afternoon, the parking lot crowded with SUVs, all being loaded with bags of mulch, stacks of landscape stones, and pots of ornamental grasses.

Heading for the exit I found myself behind an older

model pickup truck—no extra doors or wide tires or pinstripes. The driver appeared to be in his late sixties. He leaned out of the window to glance at the cargo, and I could see that his hair, though stippled with some gray, was still as dark as his skin. There was a woman in the truck with him, and I safely assumed, I think, that she was his wife. The cargo bed was empty save for one item—a yellow rosebush. Pushed up against the cab for stability, its long canes danced with the movement of the truck over the asphalt.

I couldn't help thinking of them in comparison to the other people I'd encountered in the store, the ones who live in subdivisions with restrictive covenants, the ones who read *Martha Stewart Living* and sketch garden plans on graph paper, the ones—like me—who use weed fabric and landscape pins.

Traffic on the highway was heavy, all four lanes pulsing with vehicles moving east and west. He would be careful, I knew. Careful because he remembered when this was a two-lane highway and wished it still was. Careful because he was transporting things of importance. Careful because he had reached an age at which he knew that care must be taken with everything.

When a break opened, the truck slowly moved forward over three lanes to turn left and, as it did, both of them—husband and wife—looked back to check on the rose. It was a moment of such tenderness I thought I would cry.

Stretched out on the deck in the darkness, I can see his strong hands dig the hole for the rosebush and gently place it in the ground, and I can see her standing behind him, arms crossed and head tilted in a satisfied pose. I can hear him grunt as he rises and brushes the dirt from his hands on the legs of the pants she will wash and dry and fold. I can see them walk inside together as the sun dissolves into the selvage of the day.

And I look up and see two stars, equally bright and so close together it seems as though the Big Dipper must have emptied them into the sky in the same scoop.

May 8, 2011

A tractor, a big tractor, its diesel motor droning from across a distant field. That's what it sounded like. Or a box fan, turned on high, held in place by a window sash pulled down tight on its metal frame and blowing out into the hot summer night to create a draft for the rest of the open windows in the house. That's what it sounded like. Or the jet engine of a DC-10 making its final approach to Hartsfield, its shadow an immense gray bird falling over the cars on I-75. That, too, is what it sounded like.

But it was none of those things. None of those mechanical, manufactured, man-marked sounds. The hum that swelled into the air and surged through the trees and surrounded me like a tight sweater was thousands—tens of thousands? hundreds of thousands?—of cicadas serenading themselves and anything within at least half a mile with the song they get to sing only once every thirteen years.

The friend I was visiting had warned me, but I was not prepared for the depth of the rumbling that greeted me when I walked outside into sunshine that had warmed up the cicadas enough to begin the performance. The sound vibrations were coming at me from every direction, and I could almost feel myself pulsing in time with the buzz. It was confusing and calming, discordant and melodic, repulsive and enticing, all at the same time.

Given the fact that this type of cicada appears so seldom and not at all in south Georgia, chances were that this would be my only chance to see one, so I set off into the woods at the end of the yard, scanning the landscape, certain I would be able to find one fairly easily. I did not. I scoped out the pine trees I'd been told they preferred, alert for the bulbous red eyes that distinguish them from their cousins who show up every summer. Nothing. I surveyed the undergrowth, stirring it up a little with my shoes. Still nothing.

"Oh, well," I sighed to my friend who was graciously helping me search, "at least I got to hear them." And at just that moment, that exact moment, I looked down and there, on the arm of a teak garden bench, was a cicada. A thirteen-year cicada. A cicada with eyes that looked like clown noses. A cicada with diaphanous wings that shimmered as though dusted with gold.

I picked it up. Its thin legs clamped onto my finger, I twisted and turned it in the morning sunshine and watched the light reflect off the veins in its wings. It made not a sound while all around us the cacophony played on. A moment later it surprised me how hard it was to loosen its grip from my knuckle.

My friend and I had things to do and, to be honest, it seemed almost rude to just stand there and gawk, just stand there with my head tilted first one way and then the other, just stand there like an eavesdropper. So we left.

Later, of course, I had to do a little research, had to add a few facts to the anecdotal evidence I'd collected on my own, had to legitimize my experience with that of scientists. I found out that the thirteen-year and seventeen-year cicadas are called periodical cicadas, as distinguished from the ordinary annual cicadas, and that only the males sing, producing "acoustic signals" from a structure called a tymbal that is located on the little fellows' abdomens. All very interesting.

But the best part, the piece of information that made me tremble again, just as if I'd been surrounded by a whole room full of cicadas, was this: "Periodical cicadas...belong to the genus *Magicicada*." Magicicada? Magic cicada? Really?

It's easy—when tornadoes are erasing entire towns, when gas is nearly $4.00 a gallon, when memories of 9/11 are newly stirred—to see the darkness that frames every vision, to feel the heaviness that weighs every offering, to smell the decay that accompanies every blossom, to believe that magic has died. Easy to draw the curtains, slam the doors. Seal the borders of our hearts and close down our minds. The other option—to stay open to possibility, to hang on to hope, to believe that truth will ultimately win—that's hard.

I imagine, though, that it's hard to stay underground for thirteen years, to rein in anticipation for thirteen years, to hold back a song for thirteen years. Somehow, though, the cicadas—magic cicadas—do that hard thing. And there is something in their song that makes me think we can, too.

May 22, 2011

Spring in south Georgia, I usually explain to people who are not from around here, generally lasts about three days and those three days are not always consecutive.

The pattern goes something like this: Chill and rain set in for a week followed by one gloriously sunny day in which the azaleas on Savannah Avenue burst forth like showgirls on the Las Vegas strip. The next morning, in a fit of ill-advised optimism, I wear something with short sleeves and spend the entire day shivering under a sky gray as General Lee's Traveller. The morning after brings with it hard wind and more rain that scatters and then flattens the azalea blossoms into microscope slides.

Day four dawns with a chorus of avian courtship tunes and sunlight lasering through the cracks in the window blinds. The dogwood blooms demurely lift their faces to be kissed by a breeze that smells just slightly of grass, and I stand on the sidewalk coveting the convertibles that appear about every fifth car. Days five through eight are sunny but cold, and the only thing that makes me smile is the fact that I haven't moved my winter clothes to the guest room closet yet.

The ninth day is balmy, and I decide where to eat lunch by locating a place with an open outside table. The tenth day the temperature is 85 degrees—summer has arrived, spring is gone for good.

But this year, oh, this year, we've had a real spring. One day after another of cool mornings ripening into warm afternoons and fading into pleasant evenings. One day after another of dawns that flood the fields with light like melted butter and sunsets that bleed away like old bruises. I stand outside as the air moves in gentle currents around my face, my arms, my legs, and I understand for the first time why the vocabulary of the weatherman includes the word "mild."

As much as I have enjoyed the days of repetitive atmospheric conditions, however, I'm not so certain that the animals around Sandhill have; they've been taken off guard and their behavior shows it. For example, on the way to work the other day I saw an opossum waddling along the edge of the newly plowed field just outside the front door. His fur was exactly the color of the dirt, and at first glance all I saw was the black paws and little black nose as though he were materializing bit by bit from the early morning ether. What he was doing wandering around during what should have been his sleeping hours I can't imagine.

The activity that really had me flummoxed, however, was that around the hummingbird feeder one afternoon. I had my legs stretched out and a magazine balanced in my lap when the familiar droning started. Within seconds, not one or even two, but three hummingbirds were dive-bombing the feeder at the corner of the deck. There were other feeders in the yard, all of them full, but the trio was determined to drink from a single spout on that particular one.

With a great flapping of wings and crashing of bodies they began rolling in spirals like barnstorming biplanes. One of the three flew away rather quickly toward the feeder hanging from the chinaberry tree as the remaining two continued to poke at each others' heads with their narrow beaks. The pearly greens and blues of their bodies smeared the air in wide swaths as the pitch of their hums grew higher and higher. I'd never seen anything like it.

Eventually they separated and one, the vanquished I gathered, flitted away. The victor pitched himself down toward the feeder and lowered his head to the fake plastic blossom. Getting what he wanted, he began to move away across the yard, but just as one of the other birds re-approached he abruptly altered his direction and attacked. The same sequence of events took place at least four times, enough for me to dub him The Bully and start talking to him, first trying to convince him to play nice and, finally, letting him know in no uncertain terms that his behavior was unappreciated at Sandhill and that he'd best straighten up.

I don't think he cared.

I've always thought of spring fever as a pleasant, fanciful, slightly capricious state of mind brought about by a general feeling of gratitude that yet another dark and cold winter had been survived. Apparently that was the disease in its incubation stage. Apparently the presenting symptoms of the malady are insomnia and extreme aggression. And, as humans, apparently we should be glad that spring in south Georgia usually lasts only three days.

June 5, 2011

I went out early to go running. The grass was still damp with dew that did nothing to disguise the drought. Even at 7:30, the sun was already high enough to bounce off my bare shoulders with warmth like a toaster oven. I twisted the ear buds to my iPod into my ears; maybe the sound of someone else's voice, instead of my thoughts, would induce some sort of runner's Zen.

It is never easy to run on the dirt roads at Sandhill—they are uneven and rocky in spots, irritatingly sandy in others. When it's this dry, though, and the passage of tractor and large truck tires have created the state that gives rise to the term "washboard roads," it's worse. Maintaining a rhythm is next to impossible. Zigzagging from one side of the road to the other trying to find the spot least deep in sand takes concentration away from regular breathing. Tiny rust-colored pebbles skid dangerously under the treads of your shoes, leaving you constantly one stride away from a twisted ankle.

I knew all that before I started. And still I went.

The advantage of being out that early, other than the pretty much useless attempt to beat the heat, was getting to see all the animal tracks from the evening and night before. The thin delicate Y's of bird feet had left angled seams all up and down the road, field to field, ditch to ditch. As I came across the first one, not far from the front door, I adjusted my stride to step over it, leaving the line unraveled.

The deer tracks, edges of the heart-shaped depressions indistinct in the fine sand, were thicker and wider. Their depths indicated how fast the animals had been moving and whether they had leapt over the ditch into the road or simply walked out of the field or firebreak. Deer are timid creatures and startle easily; their tracks don't always show up in a straight line. It was harder to make sure I didn't land a foot in a spot that obscured one of their steps.

At a low spot in the road I made a quick adjustment to avoid mussing a snake line even as I wondered why a snake would have been moving that early in the day.

I was nearly a mile down the road, tasting salt on my lips and wiping my forehead with the tail of my shirt, before I realized what I was doing—taking great care, at the risk of slipping on a rock or sliding in the sand, to avoid running over the footprints of the animals that had been out before me. It seemed silly. But only for a moment.

Animals don't write memoirs or create time capsules. They don't keep journals or make scrapbooks, but they do leave records of their days. Abandoned exoskeletons, shed antlers, empty cocoons. A buck scrape on a pine tree, a dropped feather, a dried nest. Hoof prints, paw prints, claw prints across a sandy road. Each is a story of a life that shared this small piece of earth with me, with us. Is it so much to imagine what that story might be?

At the bad curve I turned around. Paused. Caught my breath. Started home.

Several vehicles had passed me—my brother in his truck on the way to PoJo's, a couple of four-wheelers with enough courtesy to slow down and minimize the amount of dust I would have to breathe, a commercial pickup—and I realized as I headed back toward Sandhill that all of them had driven over the tracks. The birds'. The deer's. The snake's. Mine.

The stories had been wiped away. The history of our presence in that place on that day was lost. Whatever message might have been written in the road was now erased. There had been no intent, no malice aforethought, not even an awareness of the consequences. And yet the result was the same as if there had been.

This earth, these days, these hearts that beat within us are tender. They bear the imprint of the slightest touch. We have no choice but to watch our steps.

June 19, 2011

I really can't help it, this thing I have about words. This fascination with their power, this wonder at their flexibility, this compulsion to string them together into necklaces of sound and rhythm that sway around my neck as I walk. The way they feel spilling out of my mouth, puffs and bursts of air shaped by throat and teeth and tongue. The way they look on a page, black lines and squiggles that stand at attention, but only barely so. There is nothing quite so magical as the read, the written, the spoken word.

I am not, of course, alone in my enchantment. Not long

ago my niece Kate and I were having an Internet chat when the topic of words came up.

"I was thinking on the way to work this morning," she told me, "about the word 'sneak.' Why is it that we always want to make the past tense 'snuck'? It's not even a word."

I thought about it a minute. "You're right," I told her. "The past tense of leak isn't luck. The past tense of speak isn't spuck. Why would it seem so natural to say 'snuck'?"

We did not, I should point out, come up with an answer. There may be one. The editors of the Oxford English Dictionary, the one they've decided not to publish in book form anymore, may have some lengthy etymological history digitalized somewhere citing the use of "snuch" by Samuel Pepys in an obscure diary entry, but for Kate's and my purposes it didn't really matter. What mattered was that in the dissection and parsing, a little more of the power had been released, kind of like nuclear fission.

My friend Mary Catherine understands, too. Not long ago she sent me a novel about a girl whose name was Ella Minnow Pea. How incredibly clever! Mary Catherine is also the friend who gave me *The Professor and the Madman*. It's about the editor of the aforementioned Oxford English Dictionary and one of its main contributors, a patient in the infamous Broadmoor Insane Asylum. A book about writing a dictionary—and I found it nearly impossible to put down.

Of course, not everyone feels this way about words. This is why so many people think that correct spelling isn't important. This is why so many people use bad grammar. And profanity. These are generally the same people who are satisfied with calling a bird a bird, a tree a tree, and never wonder what kind. How can they not understand that it makes a difference?

I wish, sometimes, that I could have a conversation with someone and not diagram our sentences in my head. That I could read a magazine article without circling with a red pen phrases that sound particularly musical. That I could leave a bookstore empty-handed. I wish, sometimes, but only sometimes, that I could treat words like tools, like utilitarian items, objects that are useful but without loveliness. It would make life so much easier if I could.

Alas (Now that's word that has fallen on hard times and really is one of my favorites.), some things cannot be changed.

And while it is easy to be discouraged at the dearth of apparent word lovers in our video-gaming, iPhone-carrying, library-closing society, there was this one moment last weekend.

I got to the wedding a little later than I had planned, and most of the guests had been seated. The polite young usher asked where I would like to sit, and, at that moment, my sweet little friend Katie Anne turned from her spot on the end of an aisle and vigorously waved in my direction. "Right there will be just fine," I told him.

I settled into the pew with Katie Anne, her mom, and her older sister Madeline as the remaining guests were seated. I opened my program just as the mom gently nudged me in the ribs with her elbow and nodded toward Madeline. I leaned forward to get a look; she was hunched forward, her attention on the book in her lap. She was oblivious to everything else.

Ah. The barbarians are not yet at the gate.

July 3, 2011

The little town where Mama grew up was so small that, whenever there was a funeral, any child who wanted could leave school to attend. The church bell would ring and teachers would announce, "If you are attending the funeral today, you may leave now." Mama, whose career goal at age ten or twelve was to be a "funeral home lady," never missed an opportunity to show respect, express condolences, and observe the tricks of the trade.

On one particular day she happened to have garnered an aisle seat at the little country church where the deceased was being remembered. At the close of the sermon, the minister invited the congregation to come forward and take one last look at the dearly departed. One of Mama's classmates was walking back down the aisle and caught Mama's eye. Mama smiled.

The next day at school, everyone was talking about the fact that, God help us all, Frances Anderson smiles at funerals.

It was hard not to remember that story earlier this week as I sat in a small country church, beside two of my girlfriends and along with many others, to remember the life of another friend's mother. She was one of those women whom women of my generation know we will never be. She had strength and resilience that manifested in quiet devotion to her family and her church. Her response to any accolade was, "I've just been so blessed." It would have been easy to turn her into a caricature.

Except for one thing. You see, she reared two very human children, one of whom was a daughter who ended up, through a series of not-so-unusual circumstances, becoming a friend of mine. And then my friends and her friends started overlapping until they became our friends, and on this particular June morning there we all were—most of us sitting in the pews, but one of us standing in the pulpit.

Deborah is a gifted minister, and, with a close relationship of over thirty years on which to draw, the portrait she painted of my friend's mother was respectful and realistic. She shared stories that highlighted the talents of cooking and sewing. She emphasized faith and generosity. She mentioned the profound effect on her own life.

Then, right in the middle of an absolutely lovely eulogy, she glanced over where I and the other two were sitting, and spoke a single sentence that elicited a most un-funeral response: we laughed. Out loud. Surrounded by church members in dark suits and sensible shoes. Sitting on the second row right behind the pallbearers. Lord help us.

Later, standing outside under the noon sun, sand from the churchyard cemetery scooting its way into our high-heeled sandals, we all talked about it. Deborah had been totally nonplussed by the outburst. She shared with us that she'd suspected there might be such a reaction and that the looks on our faces had confirmed she'd done the right thing by including the slightly comic relief. That was a comfort.

And, to tell the truth, I suspect that the laughter itself was something of a comfort, a gentle reminder in the midst of unbearable sadness that the heart can still recognize and yield to humor. A call from whatever lies beyond this life to acknowledge the grief and endure the sorrow with grace. A souvenir for the pockets of those lining the creaky wooden pews, a talisman to clutch in the days to come when absence threatens to overpower sweet memory.

We sang "A Mighty Fortress" at the funeral, all four verses. The third verse goes, "The Prince of Darkness grim, we tremble not for him; his rage we can endure, for lo, his doom is sure; one little word shall fell him." And if that one little word is said with a smile or, better yet, while laughing, well, as far as I'm concerned, that's all the better. I am, after all, my mother's daughter.

July 17, 2011

Droughts have personalities. The late-blooming adolescent who appears only after hope is high and the corn is tall and then proceeds to turn the green satin fronds into cardboard tubes. The chronic melancholy who arrives on the train that picks up winter and hangs around so long that, by the Fourth of July, she's just another face in the crowd at the parade. The manic depressive that explodes the afternoon in a twenty-minute three-inch downpour and then slinks away to pout for two weeks without so much as a cool breeze. This drought, the one that presently bears down on the asphalt and the tomato plants like a panini press, the one that seems almost impossible in light of the flooding in other parts of the country, well, I'm still trying to figure her out.

She is, like all the others, selfish and megalomaniacal, but I have observed one distinctive trait: this drought has had a strange effect on the various species of wildlife around Sandhill. I saw it first in the mockingbirds, noting an exhibition of both good sense and manners as they—contrary to past behavior—didn't seem to be relentlessly ramming their heads into the windows or relieving themselves on the front porch.

Then I noticed the squirrels, dark ones, sitting on their haunches in the middle of the fields first thing in the morning and late in the afternoon. They were big enough to be prairie dogs and looked a lot like them with their tiny hands folded across their chests as though in prayer. Squirrels are not usually still, certainly not in such an exposed position, flat open acreage spread out around them on every side. And yet these seemed bothered not at all by the noise or movement of people or vehicles.

Even the deer, normally almost invisible during the summer, especially during a very dry summer, started galloping across the fields at unexpected moments. Just the other morning a doe and twin fawns stood in the road in front of my car, nonplussed at my appearance and convinced to move out of the way only after an assertive pressing of the accelerator.

The oddest occurrence of all has been the nesting of a pair of quail under the boxwoods right outside Mama and Daddy's front door. They coo almost constantly and scurry out whenever somebody approaches the front door, their fat little bottoms swaying. One afternoon I watched Daddy sitting on the deck, cracking peanuts and tossing them over the rail toward an open spot in the hedge from which the two birds would rush out to grab the shelled nuts and then dash back into the cool cover.

Strange.

If climate change is, in fact, happening—and I don't see any reason not to believe that it is—it occurs to me that this could be just the beginning. That everything we think we know about the critters that share our living space could turn out to be as useless as the 1973 edition of the World Book Encyclopedia. That the whole "they are more afraid of you than you are of them" philosophy of dealing with snakes and raccoons and assorted other varmints may need to be seriously reconsidered. That I may soon be sitting on the front porch in the rocking chair with rabbits at my feet and cardinals in my hair.

Eventually the drought will end. What should be green will be green. What has been brittle will be soft and flexible. And the animals will, most likely, revert to their ordinary personalities. They will move back into the periphery. They will stop looking me in the eye. We will startle each other again with unexpected appearances and sudden movements.

I will miss them.

July 31, 2011

The morning sunlight falls through the wooden blinds in long white rectangles onto the floor beside us. We sit at a table littered with three or four cardboard boxes of chalk. She would call them pastels, I think. The edges of the boxes are frayed and the pastels are worn down to various lengths, some of them no longer than a match.

We are speaking in low tones. Not everyone is awake yet.

She reaches for one of the pastels and holds it between her thumb and first two fingers. It is the color of the first blush of sunrise or an unshelled shrimp. She turns it sideways and swipes it deftly in two short strokes across the curve of the ripening peach she has drawn on the heavy paper.

The movement of her wrist, the swivel from left to right, the rotation of ball within socket is so slight, so finessed, that under other circumstances it would hardly be noticeable, but I can't help noticing it. I cannot see the mark of the pastel itself, but I can suddenly see peach fuzz, stubby and shimmering.

She lifts her hand, leans back in her chair, tilts her head to one side. I can tell she is pleased. I am amazed.

We have been friends for a very long time, the artist and I. We were Brownies together in second grade, beanie caps and Bridge Ceremonies, and stayed in the same Scout troop all the way through elementary school and junior high. We went to birthday parties and sleepovers and Youth Week activities. We built floats and put together yearbooks. She was with me the first time I saw the ocean, the same ocean and the same beach that lie not too far outside the window where we now sit.

She was always the artistic one. Those floats needed posters and those yearbooks needed illustrations, and she provided them in large fluorescent graphics that matched our clothes. But it wasn't until later, long after the insatiable adolescent need for group identification began to wane, that the talent coerced its way into the light. Now she paints landscapes and still lifes in colors deep and intense and nuanced. One of them hangs at Sandhill.

She holds the drawing at arms' length, lowers it, and picks up another pastel, this one darker. She makes a few strokes on the background, picks up a paper towel and buffs. The depth deepens. The two-dimensional drawing is becoming a three-dimensional image.

We talk about how she came to acknowledge her gift, the people who encouraged her. Tears fill her eyes. We talk about how hard it is for children who are different, even if it is a good different—artistically different, intellectually different. We talk about how lucky we were to have parents who loved us and loved each other. Tears fill my eyes. We talk about how easy it is for a child, anyone's child, to lose her way and how important it is to remember that they always come back to what they know. We wipe our eyes. With our hands, not with the pastel-streaked paper towel.

The drawing is done. It will be a gift for the folks who have given us this time away at their beautiful home at the beach.

"I will have to spray it with hair spray," she says. "I didn't bring any fixative."

"So I don't get to smell banana popsicle?" I ask.

My friend—my good friend, my old friend—throws back her head and laughs. Loudly. Forgetting for just a moment that not everyone is awake yet. I smile back at her, thinking that a little color and a deft touch is all it takes to turn a two-dimensional moment into a three-dimensional memory.

Laughter and tears in the early morning light of the ocean. This is the day that the Lord hath made. I will rejoice and be glad.

August 14, 2011

A couple of weeks ago the Braves played an extra-innings game. I was out of town and having my usual trouble falling asleep, so I stayed with them—propped up in the bright white sheets of the Holiday Inn—until after midnight, at which point I decided I should at least try to get some rest. At 2 a.m. I gave up and turned the television back on. They were still at it.

The game lasted nineteen innings, longer than two regulation games, and after a jolt of Diet Coke the next morning I started wondering: If, as I've long believed, baseball is the perfect metaphor for life, what does a nineteen-inning game that ends on a controversial call at home have to say?

You never know how long a baseball game is going to last. There is no clock as there is in football or basketball; the rules give each team nine opportunities to score, and when those opportunities have been used up, whoever has the most runs wins. Occasionally things get a little complicated in the later innings—a pitcher falls apart and allows the other team to catch up, a hitter comes off the bench and makes a great hit—and the game gets extended, but only for a few brief moments. Sort of like open-heart surgery or a liver transplant.

But nineteen innings? Really?

The first three innings, what poet E. Ethelbert Miller who wrote about midlife in his memoir "The Fifth Inning" would consider youth and young adulthood, were exciting. Pittsburgh took a 3–0 lead, and Atlanta came back to tie it. But nothing happened after that, and by inning 15 everybody was exhausted and their uniforms were filthy and shredded at the knees, and starting pitchers were asking for directions to the outfield because they knew that the next substitution was probably going to be sending them there.

And those of us crazy enough to still be watching were saying prayers that sounded way too much like Ricky Bobby: "Dear Lord, Baby Jesus, would you please let Martin Prado hit this next pitch over the centerfield wall, Lord, Baby Jesus? I need to turn off this light and go to sleep, but I just have this feeling that if I don't watch this game to the very end, somehow I'm going to be responsible if the Braves don't win and then lose the National League East Championship by one game to those obnoxious Phillies. And, Baby Jesus, what if they somehow don't even win the Wild Card and don't get to play in October and I have to carry that guilt for the rest of my life? Dear Lord, Baby Jesus, would you please let Martin Prado at least get a double?"

According to my calculations, based on an average life expectancy in the United States of 78.7 years, playing a 19-inning game is like living to 166. There can't possibly be any metaphorical application of that.

Except, of course, that the beauty of metaphor is its

malleability. No one lives to 166, but some people do live a very long time, and some people who live not long at all manage to fit a lot of adventure and learning and love into just a few years. And as I contemplated the statistics—life expectancy and box score—it came to me: the point of the nineteen-inning game was to impress upon me something I'd heard my favorite Braves broadcaster Joe Simpson say over and over: "Every game is different."

Every life is different. Some lives are one-run no-hitters. Some are slugfests. In one at bat you can strike out swinging, the next get hit by a pitch, and the next hit a grand slam. In one inning you can turn an unassisted triple play and in the next make a throwing error that costs your team the lead. Sometimes the weather forces the umpire to call the game in the fifth inning, and sometimes it goes nineteen. You just never know.

What you always have to keep in mind, of course, is that the only way to score, the only way to win is to be safe at home.

August 28, 2011

He was late in arriving. The lunch crowd had dispersed and the restaurant was nearly empty. The blades of the ceiling fans caught the sunlight from the glass panels in the front doors and threw tiny trapezoidal flashes at the corners of my eyes. Tall plastic glasses of tea—his sweetened the right way, mine artificially so—sweated on the table between us.

The dialogue hardly seemed natural. We were talking so quickly, anticipating each abrupt turn of the conversation and segueing from one unrelated subject to another, that an eavesdropper could have mistaken the conversation as having been scripted by one of the Ephron sisters. We laughed out loud at sentences that didn't need finishing and leaned forward on tented elbows to egg each other on in the telling of one tale after another.

Time passed too quickly and he had to go, head on down the road to the family wedding where he was expected. We walked outside toward our cars.

He stopped. "Ah, rosemary," he sighed, brushing his fingertips across the pointed stems of the plant in a large urn on the sidewalk. James is a landscape architect. He knows a thing or two about plants, including the Latin name for anything about which I've ever asked advice, so I was not surprised that he would stop and draw his fingertips up to his nose to breathe in the scent. "Don't you just love rosemary?"

Yes. Yes, I do.

"Do you grow rosemary at Sandhill?"

"Yes. I have a couple of plants." I didn't mention that I have struggled the last few years to keep those pitiful plants alive, moved them from one place to another to regulate sunlight, watered more, watered less, watered not at all—all in an effort to make them look like these full and flush specimens that guard the front doors of one of my favorite eating places.

He smiled and said, "You know, rosemary grows where strong women live."

No. No, I didn't know that.

And I couldn't stop thinking about it. I would, if anyone asked, describe myself as strong. I work hard at anything I attempt. I carry more than my weight. I've survived a blow or two. And yet my rosemary was spindly and skinny and brown on the tips. It bothered me.

A few days later I was outside playing in the yard, as my Grandmama Anderson called her gardening, contemplating how to fill the blank space at the corner of the house where Daddy had pulled up the ligustrum bush. It occurred to me that I could transplant the rosemary from the big clay pots in which they had been residing into the ground where they could keep company with the verbena and a couple of miniature gardenias.

I lugged the pots from the front porch (I told you I was strong), emptied them, loosened the roots, and dropped each of the plants into the holes I'd dug. I patted the dark dirt around their trunks and watered them well. And then I kinda sorta said a prayer, a rosemary blessing that would not be found in any missal or lectio divina. A few words along the line of, "Please, rosemary, grow."

Please, rosemary, prove that I am strong.

It's been almost six months since I put the rosemary in the ground. It is thriving. It is the color of a spruce tree just cut in December. It is full and rounded like the skirt of a ball gown. It is growing taller and its scent is deeper. When I brush my fingertips across its stems, it yields and springs back without losing any needles.

There had been nothing wrong with the rosemary. It hadn't been diseased. It hadn't been getting too much or too little light or water. It just needed to be loosed. It needed the freedom to stretch its roots beyond the artificial limits I'd unknowingly put on it.

I stand in the early evening light, leaning over the banister of the deck, staring down at the rosemary. The sounds of late summer pulse around me. I am thriving. I am full. I am growing. I can yield and spring back. I am strong. I am rosemary.

September 9, 2011

I've worked in this building for eleven years. I'm presently in my third office. The first one was directly by the front door, and everyone who passed felt compelled to come in. It had a set of double windows with a sill wide enough that, on afternoons when my brain pulsed like the walls of a disco and distraction was the only antidote for the throbbing, I could sit and watch the traffic—car and foot—move by on Main Street in currents running north and south.

There was a gingko tree right outside the window, and it marked the seasons with a local accuracy that the calendar never could. Sometimes it was the swaying of its branches in a brisk spring breeze that caught my attention and pulled me away from the mayhem documented in the files on my desk, if not so completely as to actually sit in the window, at least to prop my feet and let my face feel the warmth of the sun for a few healing moments.

I got moved from that office to one near the back stairs, an equally busy location. It had one window from which I overlooked not a gingko tree and Main Street but an alley. When I turned away from the blinking cursor, the blinking telephone, I saw not sensuous curves and nascent buds, but an overgrown courtyard in the middle of which sat an abandoned toilet and flat rooftops of varying heights—brick and concrete and tar paper. The air conditioning unit for the building next door sat on a metal platform attached to the wall of the second floor. It was rusty. The top collected water when it rained, and it rained a lot while I was in that office.

There was a bench in the courtyard. It was rusty, too. It was missing part of its back and all around it weeds grew up between the bricks. The scene both whispered and screamed loneliness.

That single window was off-kilter in its sash, and in the winter months cold air seeped through the cracks and overpowered the output of the little ceramic heater I kept under my desk to warm my feet. There was no sitting in the windowsill in this office.

The third office, the one I now occupy, is on the back corner. It is larger than the previous two and is at the end of the hallway, in a sort of interior cul-de-sac shared by only one other office and a tiny kitchen. When I close my door here, it is more likely for the purpose of climate than crowd control. The same furniture, the same books, the same certificates identify its occupant.

There are two windows, one overlooking the alley, one Main Street. My office marks the intersection where the noise and constant activity of the street crosses the quiet and emptiness of the alley. The humming of cars and trucks is set off against the non-noise of occasional foot traffic. The wide and open juts up against the narrow and constricted, and the contrast is stark.

I've been here a while. Long enough to have changed out some of the older photographs for more recent ones. Long enough to have gone through a couple of different neighbors in the office next door. Long enough to have survived the renovation of the office building across the alley, a renovation that took months and involved too many afternoons of a cement mixer underneath my window grinding and grinding at a decibel level that had me teetering on whatever decibel level is my personal pain threshold.

I've been here a while and yet, strangely enough, I've only just now come to see this place as an intersection. The single point on a graph where the Y axis, traveling in one direction, and the X axis, traveling in the other, meet. And having seen it, I'm now asking myself what exactly does one do at an intersection?

That depends, of course, on what one sees. A traffic light, a stop sign—those are easy to interpret. But what if there are no traffic signals? What if there are no street signs? What if there is an accident blocking your lane?

The answers are all the same. First, slow down. Then decide. Right, left, or straight ahead. Maybe even a U-turn if it's clear there's been a mistake. All viable options.

What is not an option is stopping. In the middle. Of the road. It is there that danger lies.

September 25, 2011

I finally used my passport. It's been in my safe for eight years, its navy blue cover stiff, the edges of its pages unruffled. It would be difficult to explain why it took so long; the important thing is that now a lovely blue stamp on one of its pages confirms the fact that my feet left the sovereign soil of the United States, landed in Ireland, and returned.

I went alone. One suitcase, a backpack, and no telephone. I visited six different cities, rode over 800 miles on various buses, and walked about 10 miles a day trying my hardest to impress upon my memory everything I saw and heard, smelled and tasted. I noticed right away that the landscape really is as green as all the PBS documentaries make it look, and the patchwork of countryside is stitched together not by fencerows but by hedges high and low.

It was jolting to see so many flowers blooming in September. All the public parks were flush with roses, hydrangeas, and pansies. At a street flower market in Dublin I found Gerbera daisies the color of strawberry ice cream, and I took I don't know how many photographs of window boxes spilling over with asters, impatiens, and petunias.

I hiked six and a half miles through the Gap of Dunloe in the Killarney National Park, countryside that made me feel like a character in a nineteenth-century novel. There were huge sheep, close enough to touch, grazing on the hillsides waterfalls and brooks, miles and miles of unbroken rolling hills, and wildflowers in colors that came out of a Sharpie pack.

At the Trinity College Library I stood in line to see the Book of Kells, the illuminated manuscript of the four Gospels written in Latin and created by Celtic monks around A.D. 800 It is art and inspiration and perseverance made concrete. Staring at the words written in ink made from minerals on vellum made from calfskin, I tried to imagine the men whose life's work it was, day after day, to create this monument to

God. Did they ever wonder whether what they were doing was worth the effort?

I carried that question with me as I arrived at Shannon Airport early on Saturday morning, not at all looking forward to the twenty-three hours of travel time ahead of me, in clothes that you could tell I'd been wearing off and on all week, and just a tad concerned about being in an airplane on the day before the tenth anniversary of 9/11.

I had cleared the second level of security and was in the waiting area outside customs, the last gauntlet to run before boarding the airplane. There weren't many people at that hour of the morning, a few folks reading newspapers and drinking coffee, a few browsing in the last outpost of the duty-free store. I wandered through the aisles of refrigerator magnets and chocolate bars trying to figure out how to spend my last few Euros, constantly glancing at the plastic watch on my wrist to see how much time had passed.

I moved a little closer to the departure door and noticed that a significant number of American soldiers had begun walking through the terminal. They were all dressed in desert combat fatigues and moved singly and in small groups toward a large set of gray double doors near the exit I would use when I went through customs. A few of them lingered in the hard plastic seats of the waiting area. Some just stood and chatted quietly with each other.

I found myself standing next to three of them. One was tall, square-shouldered. His Army haircut was salt-and-pepper. I'd guess he was in his early forties, most assuredly an officer.

"There are a lot of y'all here today," I offered. "Headed home or going somewhere else?"

"Kuwait," he said. And, after looking over at the other two, "Then other places."

I felt something rise in my belly, a knot of emotion that caught me completely off guard and climbed rapidly into my chest and then into my throat. My eyes welled up with tears as

I heard myself choking out, "Thank you."

He looked me dead in the eye, straightened his shoulders a little, and said in the steadiest voice I have ever heard, "It is an honor to serve."

A few moments later he and the others gathered their things and started toward the double doors. The prayer I whispered was as much for the mothers and wives and daughters as for them.

The world is full of monks and soldiers, those who approach their task with reverence and awe. Those who gladly accept, but do not need, the affirmation of others in order to march into the fray, face down the foe. Those who know there is no weight in bearing what is right.

I have thought about him, the soldier, every single day since I returned home.

Like the monks who spent their entire lives copying the scriptures, like the soldiers who were being deployed, none of us can ever know if our efforts will meet with success. Whether we direct our passions toward preserving history or defending freedom, rearing children or building a business, the motivation cannot be derived solely from what we think might be the end result. Somewhere in the midst of the preserving and defending and rearing and building, a man, a woman, must be able to find the honor that it is to serve.

October 5, 2011

The sun this morning is a cross-section of pink grapefruit back-lit by a strobe light. It balances on the horizon, pulsing and trembling with the tension of anticipation, as though the day cannot begin quickly enough. As the road curves, it moves back and forth like the bouncing ball on the old Mitch Miller television show, and I find myself wishing desperately that I knew the song. I try to identify what I am feeling and I settle on wistfulness.

KATHY A. BRADLEY

The summer has faded too quickly. The pale pink blooms on the cotton plants outside my back door that just days ago could have passed, at a distance, for tightly closed peonies, have popped like popcorn into thick white bolls. The rabbits have made their seasonal dine-and-dash into the hosta bed, leaving behind gnawed stems that splay out like the hair on a cartoon Einstein. The sycamore tree has dropped its first feeble leaves.

In a couple of days I will have a birthday. Is it possible that the wistfulness is not for the summer, but for something else?

I hear myself telling people that I will turn fifty-five and wonder about the source of that particular colloquialism. The verb "turn" has so many different meanings—to change direction or allegiance, to rot or become rancid, to injure by twisting, to change color, to move around, to divert or deflect. None of them makes much sense in the context of getting older.

Last year, when I turned fifty-four, I decided that before I gained another year I would do fifty-five things I'd not done before. There was no checklist; the point was to be open to newness and change and adventure in an intentional way and trust that life would bring me experiences that would, in the words of Walter Cronkite, alter and illuminate my times.

So, in the last year I have, among other things, given blood, eaten an oyster, served Communion, attended a drive-in movie and a Jewish worship service (within twelve hours of each other), run a road race, talked in my sleep, finally climbed the lighthouse on St. Simons, and taken the hunter safety course. I also ate kale, collards, sushi, and a tomato I grew myself. I spent a Saturday night riding in a police cruiser, signed a book contract, and went to Europe.

The point, of course, was not the number itself or even reaching the goal (which I did with one week to spare). The point was to get to that next birthday and not simply be a year older, but a year wiser, wider, deeper, stronger. And I am. I know things, feel things, can do things that I did not know, had not felt, could not do a year ago. I have broadened my perspective and narrowed my focus. I, at long last, have an idea of what I am capable of being.

"Some things just come by birthdays," Daddy says. Including, I can now say, the value of birthdays themselves.

Within minutes the pink grapefruit sun has floated up into the sky like a helium balloon escaped from a toddler's fist. It is smaller, more yellow. Its light is less shimmery. It is no longer daybreak but early morning. And soon early morning will yield to day, which will, in turn, give way to high noon. The round circle in the sky will move, will change size and color, will cast shadows and erase them completely before slinging them in the opposite direction. It will move all the way across the wide and wondrous sky before it silently slips from sight.

Is that, I wonder, what it is to turn fifty-five or whatever age is the next number up? Is it simply moving from one place to another in a graceful arc? Is it at long last recognizing oneself as a sun, not a moon, a body capable of producing its own heat and light? Is it finally, finally realizing that the changing size, the changing color, the presence or absence of shadows is nothing more than the illusions of those who watch from the ground?

I think I know the song now. Summer has faded. But autumn, golden autumn, is on its way.

October 23, 2011

The fog thins just enough for me to see the sun, a flat white Communion wafer floating in a halo of wavy opalescence. The trees and fences and barns beneath it stand unusually straight, as though three dimensions are not enough to spotlight their long lines and sharp angles. My hand on the steering wheel moves left and right, in the easy rhythm of a weaver's shuttle, following the curves of the road toward that flat white sun onto which it is easy to believe that, if I just keep going, I could slide like a base runner stealing home.

It is a morning for contemplation. No radio news or iPod music. No telephone calls to return or mental lists to make. Just breathing. And looking around. And wondering.

I was reading the other day about caribou. Most of the world (and North Americans during the month of December) call them reindeer. They have specialized noses that warm cold air before it reaches their lungs and hooves that adapt to the season. They are believed to be the only mammals that can see ultraviolet light.

The caribou are migratory animals, and some populations travel up to 3,100 miles a year covering 390,000 square miles, the furthest of any terrestrial mammal. The ones who live near the Arctic Circle follow the same migration path every year, an innate sense of some kind drawing them into the footsteps of their forebears. Also drawn to this same path year after year are the coyotes that feed on the caribou, which patiently and lazily lie in wait for the inevitable buffet.

One would think—if one were, say, driving into town on a foggy autumn morning and being more successful than usual at keeping at bay one's own mental coyotes—that the caribou would eventually, maybe not this year or next year, but over a few caribou generations, figure out the need to change that path, to shake things up a bit in order to preserve the population. One could imagine, without much effort, the old bulls, slower but wiser, lowering their five-foot wide antlers and nudging the calves toward a detour. One might think that, if they didn't, being able to preheat their oxygen or see in the dark wouldn't amount to much more than parlor tricks for some future reindeer diaspora.

There is a legend that says the caribou are what keep the earth turning. That over the millennia their hooves have worn a deep crown into the top of the world. That they run, pounding into the ground at 50 miles per hour, regardless of what stands in their way, including the coyotes, because if they stop so will the planet. There is, says the recounter of the legend, "an inner necessity that outweighs all consequence."

I have had a number of difficult conversations lately with someone who is dear to me, someone who has loved me for a long time. There are things about which we disagree. Not inconsequential things, but important things, heart things. My dear one does not understand some of the choices that I have made, does not understand that, in fact, they were not choices at all, but simply the outward manifestation of an inner necessity.

I have tried to explain. I have not succeeded. All that the dear one sees are the consequences, the coyotes crouched in the shadows by the side of the path I've chosen and the scars left by the ones that came along before.

I notice that the fog has cleared a bit. The sun has warmed to margarine yellow and grown larger as it topped the pine trees that trim the cotton fields. It is easier to see the other cars and trucks in the herd headed toward town. Fog, it should be noted, disperses more easily than hard feelings.

We are all migratory animals. The food and shelter we seek may not be literal and the seasons we follow may be emotional rather than calendar ones, but every ear has heard a call that will not be silenced. Every heart has sensed a purpose that will not be ignored. I know this because, despite the coyotes, the earth keeps turning.

And the fog always disappears.

November 6, 2011

Two more ligustrum are gone, the two that guarded either side of the front steps. They were well over six feet tall, too tall for me to trim from the ground, too dangerous to try to trim leaning off the porch, so they constantly sported asymmetrical spikes of bright yellow and neon green that made them look like herbaceous rock stars.

I'd struggled with the decision for a long while. These two, unlike the one I'd dispatched back in February, had not come to me from a nursery in a tub of thin black plastic, but from Tattnall County in a fertilizer bucket of thick white plastic. Skinny but tough little cuttings from Grandmama's yard, she'd sent them home with Mama one day, ever convinced that anybody, even I, could make things grow.

Other than the two ligustrum, which I did manage to keep alive and see turn into sturdy fat sentries defending the entry to Sandhill, the only thing I have that belonged to Grandmama is the iron bed in the guest room. But Grandmama was a pragmatist, and had she known the misery that ligustrum pollen inflicts upon my respiratory system, she would have looked at me, arms folded across her cotton print shirtwaist, and said, with just a bit of incredulity that the thought had not occurred to her educated granddaughter, "Pull 'em up."

So we did.

Well, actually, Daddy did. But before the extraction, we—like country people do—stood and stared for a few minutes. Stood with our hands on our hips and stared at the bushes, at the steps they'd begun crowding, at the rocking chairs they hid from view. And when we had stared long enough, we bounced our chins in nods of satisfaction and confirmation that, yes, pulling up these bushes was, in fact, a good thing.

"I'll go get the tractor and the chain," Daddy said, and in a few minutes he was back with the chain and a tractor three times as big as he needed because it was the only one without a plow or something else hitched to it at the moment.

I couldn't tell you where the chain came from or how long Daddy's had it. There's never been but the one, as we say, and, unlike so many things around the farm that tend to get misplaced or broken or used up, the chain just always is. Ferrol Sams wrote, "In the beginning was the land. Shortly thereafter was the father." And, in my mind, sometime no later than the second or third day was the chain, already rusted to a dark river red.

The chain has pulled fallen pine trees from across the road, vehicles of various sorts from whatever spot they had broken down, and, at least once, a corn combine from a grown-over ditch where Daddy inadvertently drove it while trying to turn for the next pass. Years ago when our horse Sonny suddenly died one day from a congenital heart defect, the chain pulled him to his grave.

On this day, Daddy looped the chain around the trunk of the ligustrum, clicked the hook into one of the links, and jumped back onto the tractor where a quick thrust of diesel power ripped the roots from their place in the soil. Quick. Easy. Satisfying.

The tractor moved away, leaving a wide curving wake across the front yard where the branches of the bush scraped across the already browning grass, and I saw the landscape open up, the view from the porch that had been obstructed like some of the seats in old Shea Stadium suddenly clear and wide and bright in the autumn sunshine.

I could sit in the rocking chair and see the mailman pull up to my mailbox. I could see all the way across the field to the spot where the deer come out in the late evening to eat. I could see farther than I'd seen in years.

We don't often think of chains as beneficial. They fasten. They hold down. They rattle loudly while the Jacob Marleys of our pasts haunt our days with endless replays of scenes that didn't work and scripts that need rewriting. They bind us with the strength of alloy steel to people and places and jobs that restrict movement and leave us atrophied and pale.

But sometimes chains are just what we need. A chain can

clear your path or pull you home when you're broken. A chain can turn you around and bury what needs burying. And, when you're ready to let go, a chain can open up a whole new way of seeing.

November 20, 2011

November Sunday. Two words that, together, do not ordinarily conjure up images of bare feet and air-kiss breezes. And, yet, on this November Sabbath, the sun that is growing more visibly distant each day seems to have slipped back into the parlor with a wink and a flirtatious smile for one final curtsy to summer.

I am driving Daddy over to the Waters place to move a tractor. Not an ox-in-the-ditch kind of thing. More a good-reason-to-be-out-in-the-sunshine kind of thing. Cotton fields rimmed by maple trees in the height of fall flame remind me of candy canes, the Canadian flag, Santa's suit. There should be a better word than vivid.

I am tempted to roll down the windows, but, temperature notwithstanding, it is still fall, there is still pollen, and Singulair ain't cheap.

When we get to the field, Daddy asks me to wait until he gets the tractor cranked. Apparently there is some reason to believe it might not start. He hops into the cab, grabs an unusually long screwdriver, and hops back down. The engine cover on the tractor opens like a coffin. The inside is a dark and oily conglomeration of cylinders and coils.

He thrusts the screwdriver into the belly of the beast like a dagger. The target appears to have been a cylinder wrapped in a coil.

"What are you doing?" I ask.

"Bleeding out the air. There's a teeny little leak somewhere in the line. Haven't had the time to fix it, so just have to bleed it out to crank it."

The absence of a subjective pronoun doesn't bother me so much as the idea of bleeding air. It doesn't sound right. Bleeding involves blood, not air. And bleeding is, as a general rule, not something one does deliberately.

The diesel engine coughs, catches, settles into the syncopated rhythm that is as soothing to me as a lullaby. The engine cover falls with a tinny clank and Daddy lifts his hand to release me from my post. He is back in the cab with one springing step, and by the time I reach the field gate, he's right behind me headed home.

I watch him in my rear-view mirror for a couple hundred yards then turn onto the paved road, headed toward the recycling center where I will empty the back of the Escape of bins of magazines and newspapers and plastic bottles and aluminum cans in my small attempt at some kind of penance for my consumption. Even when he is out of view, I am still thinking about bleeding air.

In the context of mechanical engineering, it is obviously a positive thing, a remedy for an ill, but I can't shake the feeling that in the context of living it is anything but.

In the Genesis story of creation it is the breath of God that introduces Adam's soul into the clay sculpture that is his body, and most other cultures and religions also invoke the breath as that which carries life. We acknowledge the power of an experience or the beauty of an object by saying that it takes our breath away. It is with breath, with air, that we speak, that we sing, that we kiss. It is how each of us demonstrates our unique humanity. Surely there is no legitimate reason for its being deliberately bled away.

Except, of course, I realize with a suddenness that causes my eyes to widen, when you've been holding your breath. When you've been living in limbo. When you've been sitting on a fence so long that you've worn the wood smooth and can't feel the splinters anymore. Because when that is where you are, it just may take a screwdriver jabbed into the coils of your chest to force out the stale air so the fresh can get in.

And at that point, the best you can do is pray that the farmer with the screwdriver is someone you trust.

December 4, 2011

I am standing at the kitchen window, staring into darkness where only a few minutes before the light had smeared lavender across the horizon like a little girl's first attempts at makeup. It is the night before Thanksgiving, the dishwasher has died, and one by one each knife, spoon, spatula, pot, plate, bowl, cup, and colander involved in the preparation of my assigned dishes, together with all the dirty glasses and plates and silverware that filled the dishwasher at the time of its demise, must be washed and dried by hand.

The onions and celery and peppers, diced delicately into small green cubes and tossed with the shoe-peg corn and the bright red pimientos, await the marinade that is cooling on the back burner and tomorrow's verdict of whether Jenn's morning sickness will subside long enough for her to enjoy it. Aunt Doris's lime congealed salad, without which no holiday meal is complete, is congealing in the refrigerator, filled with nuts that Mama and Daddy picked up from under the tree in the side yard and shelled while watching Fox News. The nuts have also made their way into half of the fudge, the other half left nut-less for Katherine. The cranberry salad will be finished once it thickens enough for the pineapple and yet more nuts to be stirred in.

The satisfaction of completion makes up for the frustration of the dishwasher's untimely death, and I am unexpectedly content as I lower my hands into the hot sudsy water. Dishcloth in right hand, bowl in left, I swoosh the water around and around, set a rhythm for the task and for my breathing. Cooler water pours out of the long neck of the faucet and washes away the suds, leaves the bowl clean. Its curved glass sides reflect the overhead light in a starburst that causes me to blink. I turn it upside down onto the striped cotton dishtowel that stretches down the counter. Lines of water run down its face like tiny rivers racing to the sea.

I reach carefully to the bottom of the sink, beneath the suds, feel around for the knives, pull one up by its handle, wipe its teeth free of the celery strings. I add more hot water to help melt the tiny shards of chocolate left in the bottom of the pot. Each utensil, each dish requires its own attention, its own particular touch of my hand to be made clean. I am struck at some point how like a baptism this all is—going down dirty, coming up clean.

It doesn't take much for that train of thought to move right on down the track to see the rest of the Thanksgiving preparation as sacrament as well. Take and eat this bread. Take and eat this marinated vegetable salad, this fudge, this turkey and dressing and pecan pie. And do it in remembrance of me. Do it in remembrance of all that has been good in your life, all that is good in your life, all that will be good in your life.

In the drawer by the sink are more striped cotton dishtowels. I get out another one and begin drying the dishes, piled on the counter in a precarious pyramid of glass and plastic and stainless steel. The last traces of water on the bowls, the spoons, get absorbed into the towel. The cabinets and drawers fill—glasses lined up, plates stacked, silverware sorted.

The darkness outside the window has grown thicker. I can make out no shapes and yet I continue to stare as I drain the sink, spray it with Fantastik, and wipe away the last vestiges of what will be my Thanksgiving offerings. I am not looking at, but toward. Maybe through.

I am wondering if it is all sacrament. Every day, not just holiday. Every meal, not just Thanksgiving. Every breath. Every blink. Every scent and sound. I am wondering if I have approached life, all of it, with the holy awe it deserves. I am wondering if I have any idea of how to be grateful.

December 18, 2011

I first noticed it on Sunday—a sycamore leaf, the size of a spread hand and the color of cured tobacco, stuck in the stems of a cotton plant at the edge of the driveway. Surprisingly, it was still there Wednesday morning, having withstood a couple days of stiff wind and one day of sustained rain. Obviously, I was meant to take note. I got out of the car and walked to the edge of the field for a closer look.

A picked-over cotton field looks like a phalanx of badly drawn stick figures. Nearly every stalk has at least one boll left that looks like a head with tufted white hair escaping from its hard brown helmet, and the various angles at which the spindly stems pierce the air make it appear as though the infantry is advancing at full speed, spears and pikes flailing at the ends of skinny arms. This one, though, the one cradling the sycamore leaf in its arms like a placard, seemed to be less warrior, more prophet. And the question becomes, I thought to myself, what has it been sent to proclaim?

I got back into the car, squinted my eyes into the rising sun, and headed toward town. As I rounded what we call the bad curve, the bag of Christmas gifts I'd placed in the floorboard fell over and squished, I was sure, their carefully tied red and white bows. Using one hand to maneuver between the ditches while I leaned across the front seat trying to reach and right the bag, I muttered, "Why do I always do this? I knew when I put it there it would probably tump over! I knew it and did it anyway! What made me think that the law of centripetal force was going to be suspended just for me?"

It was not the first time I've had that conversation with myself. Not even the first time that morning. I regularly try to do too much with too little and move too fast for too little and, as a result, have proven over and over again that Newton's laws of motion, among other things, are called laws for a reason.

Both hands back on the steering wheel, I took a deep breath, reminded myself that squished ribbon would not make any difference to the children who would open those packages later in the day, and watched the still dew-wet landscape slide swiftly past the car windows.

But the cotton plant prophet would not leave me alone. He kept crying out in the wilderness at the edge of my mind as I greeted my coworkers, turned on the computer, read the newspaper. He kept hoisting that sycamore leaf above his head and shouting, "Behold!" He kept staring at me as if at any moment he was going to have to declare me, in all my stubborn ignorance, a viperous Pharisee.

I finally conceded my ground, took my second deep breath of the morning, and leaned back in my chair to stare out the window at the gingko tree, its golden leaves a thousand mirrors of clear winter sunlight. I did not have to close my eyes to re-conjure the morning's encounter: sycamore leaf, dry and brittle, turned on its side and captured in the defoliated stems of a dead and abandoned cotton plant.

Look again, the prophet said. Look more closely at the leaf dry and brittle. It is whole, not one lobe or rib broken. It was lifted by the wind from the ground to which it had fallen, carried gently to this spot, and left to drop again. In its first descent, from the tree where it grew, it was aging but still supple. It was easy for it to fall and remain in one piece. The second fall should have broken the leaf, but it didn't.

The laws of nature being what they are, the leaf should have torn along its veins like perforated paper. Its thin edges should have caught on the sharp bracts and broken into bronze-colored dust. Its smooth blade should have cracked like dried mud. But, miraculously, it did not.

I laughed out loud. Of course. It is Christmas. The season of miracles. The season when virgins have babies and stars become GSP devices, when angels speak English and astronomers outsmart kings, when things fall without breaking.

Finally! said the prophet, stopping just short of calling me rebellious and stiff-necked. But there is one more thing: Christmas is the season of miracles, but it is also the season of prophecy. You need not concern yourself with the nature of the leaf—whether it is prophecy foretold or fulfilled—only with the imperative that in order to see either you must watch.

December 29, 2011

It was early. The sky was a solid gunmetal gray. The rain smelled like summer rain, light and a little musty. It fell softly and met the concrete lip of the carport like the skirt of a ball gown lowered over satin shoes. A womb outside a womb, the morning pulled me from the warmth and stillness of the house into the cool and stillness of the day.

It was early. Only one set of tire treads caught the headlights in the slick mud of road ahead of me. Only one set of tire treads, one set of eyes had come this way before me in the early dawn. I felt the pull of the siren ditches—subtle and slight—beneath my hands curved like C-clamps around the top of the steering wheel.

It was early. And wet. Too early and wet for deer to be moving, but vigilance is not easily loosed and so my eyes watched the edges, all the edges, alert to the slightest twitch of tightly muscled flank or the slightest glint of doe eye.

Ahead and to the left, through the lace of bare-limbed forest, I saw light, artificial light. Blue-white halogen. Cold and clear. Unnaturally bright. Too high to be headlights. Too low to be a plane. Shop lights, that's what they were. Shop lights at the farm on the highway. Of course.

Except that if anyone had asked me, in the exact moment before the lights broke through the almost-day to point in the direction of the shop, the highway, I would have pointed straight ahead. If someone had asked for directions I would have said, "Stay on this road and go straight ahead."

But the road isn't straight. It curves sharply to the left at a spot known as the beaver pond or, more usually, the bad curve. The curve where, in weather like this, cars and trucks driven by the most careful and experienced drivers have slid into the ditch with the smoothness of butter melting on pancakes. The curve where years ago Daddy was one of the first to arrive at an accident that left three people dead and two more seriously injured. The curve where, no matter how many times you've navigated it from either direction, you always catch your breath and feel your heart clutch when you meet another car.

This time there was no other car. This time I maneuvered my traction-less vehicle across the skim of mud through the curve to the straightaway where the lights were, suddenly, directly ahead. Funny how that happens.

I don't, as a general rule, think much of New Year's resolutions. Declaring, in the high tide of a celebratory moment, that I will henceforth do something that no previous moment has motivated me to do, or no longer do something that no previous moment has motivated me to discontinue, has always seemed a little self-righteous. Pronouncing that I will become a better something-or-other invites judgment from pretty much anyone as to whether I was any good at the something-or-other to begin with and also whether my efforts at improvement amount to much. Proclaiming that I will engage in some action or behavior with more or less frequency begs me to elevate the manifestation over the impetus, the form over the substance.

And yet, on this late December morning, another year fading in the rear-view mirror that reflects plumes of red-brown mud spraying up into the blue-gray morning, I find myself making promises, if not exactly resolutions. I promise that the road I follow will always be the road straight ahead, but with all the curves and detours and dead ends that aren't yet visible. I promise that I will watch out for the places where the deer are daring and the ditches are deep. And I promise that, no matter how many times I find it necessary to travel any given stretch, I will never try to navigate by memory alone.

Like all who write what they remember,
I am inventing the truth.

Barbara Brown Taylor, *An Altar in the World*

January 15, 2012

Order. The arrangement or disposition of people or things in relation to each other according to a particular sequence, pattern, or method. A state of proper readiness or preparation or arrangement.

Rhythm. A strong, regular, repeated pattern of movement or sound. Movement or variation characterized by the regular recurrence or alternation of different quantities or conditions, as in the *rhythm* of the tides.

Order and rhythm, the compass and sextant of my days.

The holidays were over. The tree had been struggled back into the corner of the attic where it would lie peacefully in pieces until next December. The refrigerator and pantry, the cake plate and cookie jar had been cleared of the food that appears only once a year. The green-leaved and red-berried branches, dried into crumbling tinder, had been tossed into the edge of the field to further fade and decompose. Order had been restored.

Rhythm, however, was still eluding me. The days and nights of holiday activities that disrupt, however cordially, the tempo of life had ended, but I remained off-balance, out of kilter, emotionally and mentally disoriented to the new year.

I decided to go to the gym. On the treadmill, my feet would adopt a stride of hard and steady steps, my lungs would draw in air and force it back out, my elbows would move back and forth like side rods on a locomotive. I would actually feel my heart beating inside my chest. Exercise would be my metronome.

But I got detoured. Two big diesel trucks and an excavator had arrived at the farm to remove the burned-out shell of the cotton picker that, for the last week or so, had stood sentry at the exact spot at the edge of the field where it had flamed then smoldered. Every morning and afternoon I'd passed it, stopping a couple of times to take photographs, changing my mind about what it looked like—a prop from an apocalyptic movie set? a prop from a dinosaur movie set?—and feeling a bit forlorn that I hadn't been there to see the conflagration.

With a somewhat childish delight I noticed Daddy standing just off the road in the bedraggled rows of picked-over cotton, observing the reclamation. If he could watch, so could I. For a few minutes. And then I'd get to the treadmill.

The two of us, arms folded, gave a respectful distance to the two men whose job it was to clear all evidence of the fire that had triumphed over 70,000 pounds of metal. There was a lot of incremental raising and lowering, pushing and pulling, stretching out and pulling back in of the excavator arm, making the whole process look like nothing so much as a Pixar movie projected large across the January sky and underscored by a soundtrack of diesel engine and hydraulic pump. The power line strung directly over the picker added dramatic tension.

At the two-and-a-half-hour mark, with not much apparent progress having been made, my attention wandered. I reached down to break off an unpicked cotton boll, swaying in the unseasonably warm breeze at the end of its brown chopstick of a stem. I pulled the boll from its star-pod and began rolling it between my fingers, felt the hardness of seeds hidden in the whiteness. Dividing my attention between the men wrestling with the machine and the seeds bound tightly in the soft white fibers, I extricated one, two, three…fourteen seeds.

"Can these be planted?"

Daddy interrupted his careful supervision of the two men and glanced quickly at my upturned palm, cupped to hold the fuzzy seeds.

"Oh, yeah." Ginned and cleaned, he explained, those very

seeds could eventually make their way back into the ground to start the cycle all over again. A cycle with a rhythm that is old and enduring, sure and certain, regular and reliable. A rhythm that allows for drought or disease or a cotton picker that catches fire and lights up the sky like the county fair, all without missing a beat.

I closed my fist on the cottonseeds, took a deep breath of warm winter air, and felt the gentle pump pump pump of my heart feeling its way back into rhythm with its world.

January 29, 2012

The nest is delicately balanced between two branches of one of the sawtooth oaks Adam planted at the edge of the yard eight years ago. At just about eye level, I have to ease up onto my tiptoes a bit for the right angle to see into its depths, to make sure that it is empty. It could not be more symmetrical if its avian architect had used computer-aided drafting—a cup-shaped scoop of twigs and thread-sized roots perfectly built for what? Two eggs? Three?

The ends of some of the twigs are clean-cut, sliced flat and even, and I wonder if they are the remains of logs trimmed with the chain saw and stacked up to be burned. Most of the twigs, of course, are raw and ragged, broken by wind or rain or squabbling squirrels. I can identify some of them by their bark—sycamore, scrub oak, no pine. Others have had their bark stripped away to reveal striations that look like veins pumping brown blood.

Caught in a fork in the outside edge is a leaf, bruised bronze and veined white. Dewdrops, fat and tremulous, reflect the winter-morning light that is at my back. A tiny ruffle of pale green lichen trims one of the larger outside twigs, a surprisingly stark contrast to the browns and grays of the other building materials. Birds recognize colors, don't they? Was the pastel accent intentional?

It is late. I should have already left for work and I've spent long enough staring. It is, after all, only a nest. And an abandoned one at that.

I walk back across the yard, prizing my 3-inch heels out of the soft ground with some effort. The image of the nest—the colors and textures, the way it seems to hover—shimmers like the after flash from an old Instamatic camera, and as I get into the car, one leg in, the other still balanced on its thin heel, I grasp the thought that has just raced across my mind like a news bulletin: Abandoned. The nest is abandoned.

Like a rusted-out car, a falling-down house, a foundling on a doorstep, it has been left behind, carrying the weight of ending and loss and unrealized potential. Whatever eggs were laid there are long gone. It will not be used again to nurture fledglings. Eventually the elements will weaken the careful mechanical engineering employed by its builder and the building materials will scatter on the ground beneath the tree.

Yet, it has captured me. Captured me like nothing has in days. Beauty captures. And the nest, with its delicate rough-ness, its flawless imperfection, and, yes, even its emptiness that feels like nothing so much as anticipation, is beautiful.

I shake my head at the paradoxical thought, that something abandoned can be beautiful. That something forsaken, no longer wanted, damaged and/or worn could possess a particular loveliness. That something unobtrusive and easily missed, something without obvious value, could be aesthetically pleasing.

Plato thought that all beautiful objects incorporated proportion, harmony, and unity. The universal elements of beauty, as perceived by Aristotle, were order, symmetry, and definiteness. I doubt, as I drive into the rising sun, that my nest (I have, in an unconscious act of benefaction, assumed guardianship) qualifies as beautiful under the Greek ideal.

It doesn't matter. I have learned that beauty is an

idiosyncratic concept. The eye of the beholder and all that. What the eye beholds the heart answers, and my heart has answered that this object, this fragile creation by an unidentified artisan, this nest—this abandoned nest—is beautiful.

This morning, this bright and clear January morning, that is all I know on earth and all I need to know.

February 9, 2012

The habit developed slowly, as all habits do, and morphed over the years into something more like a ritual: On the night of the full moon, just before bed, I walk out on the deck to tilt my head, stretch my neck, and gaze. Once every twenty-eight days or so, I reach out with my eyes for a touchstone, a reminder that some things remain true.

Last night I stepped onto the damp wood planks barefoot, felt the pads of my feet immediately grow chilled, and, with a slight shudder, tightened the sash on my fuzzy pink bathrobe. I took a few steps to center myself on the platform and turned toward the southeast. There it was.

I have compared a full moon to many things over the years—a poker chip being a favorite—all of them round and clean-edged. This moon, viewed through uncorrected near-sightedness, was anything but. Its perimeter changed with every blink, curving back and forth, its volume waxing and waning like a lung. I decided it look like nothing so much as a poaching egg.

Satisfied with the souvenir of a perfect image, I allowed myself a sigh of contentment. But I wasn't content. The ritual of the full moon involves not just locating it, affixing it squarely in the firmament over Sandhill. It involves words. It requires that I speak to the moon, that I acknowledge its faithfulness in appearing once again. And this time there were no words.

In the branch behind the house a sound rose up. It did not startle me; I am accustomed to the night sounds of farm and field. But it did surprise me. It was the sound of frogs. An amphibian basso profondo echoing out from the boggy edges of the pond. The sound that I can't ever remember hearing in February, the sound that usually accompanies the mild breezes of April or maybe a warm March.

My head tilted toward what was a rising chorus—now with baritones and tenors joining in. The branch that had been completely silent when I walked outside was now pulsing with voices, sound waves surging like an advancing army past the leafless branches and into the navy blue sky.

My own voice still silent, I went back inside where thin strips of moonlight fell through the cracks in the blinds across a bed in which I would eventually sleep.

I woke up early. The moon had moved to the other side of the house, was pasted in one of the panes of the bay window in the kitchen, and it reminded me that I'd left things unfinished. There are only so many full moons in a lifetime, I once wrote, and now I'd squandered one.

Regret is rarely useful. I know that. And yet sometimes I find myself determined to wrestle with it until my hip is out of joint and I can forever walk with a limp as punishment. And I might have done that this time but for the sudden realization that the words don't always have to be my own.

Standing there on the deck, feeling nothing except my toes going numb, I had assumed that the only words worth offering were the ones that I could mint. And that if the vein had gone dry then I must be silent. But the compline offered up by the frogs enveloped every creature under the moon—the deer leaving valentine-shaped footprints in the soft sand of the driveway, the owl perched in the crook of the burned-out pine tree, and the barefoot woman with arms crossed tightly across her heart. The reverberative chant without translation was all the offering of gratitude, all the acknowledgment of grandeur, all the demonstration of grace for which any life could hope.

February 22, 2012

It is Tuesday afternoon. I arrive home to find Mama and Daddy immersed in the project of burning off some under-growth in the branch behind Sandhill. I am planning a party and they've decided—actually Mama has decided—that the place will look prettier without the dead vines and fallen-over trees blocking sight of the pond. Within minutes there are three or four piles of brittle branches and broken limbs stacked into pyres, throwing fat orange flames into the late afternoon air.

Over the next couple of hours the flames eat up the piles of dead wood and, finally sated, die down, leaving matte black scars at the far edge of my yard. Already I have a better view of the still, flat water of the pond, silver-plated with the light of the sun that is fading in time with the embers.

It is Wednesday morning. Ash Wednesday. I wake up in darkness. Shower, dress, make the bed, realize I've not decided what I will undertake as a Lenten discipline. For some reason the idea of "giving up" something—chocolate, caffeine, list-making—doesn't feel right this year. For some reason and for the first time, the connotation that comes to mind has to do with "giving up" hope, and that feels contrary to the whole idea of this spiritual journey to the cross.

I go into the bathroom to put in my contacts, brush my teeth. I don't have to decide until I get to church tonight, I tell myself. There is still time. Something will come to me. I put up my hair, put on my makeup. Yes, I have all day. Something will come to me.

And then it does. Through the half-open blinds I see the topmost edge of the sun cracking the horizon across the way toward Miss Dottie's and the Indian cemetery. It is as thin and curved as the liner I have just so carefully drawn across my eyelids. It is the color of Mercurochrome and it is pulsing like a hammer-hit finger.

I sit down and watch it. It is moving. Rising, we call it, though we know that's not what is happening. Imperceptibly the arc grows larger and the color brighter, and what had been silhouettes on the landscape grow another dimension. I time travel forty days hence and see Easter, sense the expectation of things that break open and spill amazement into the world, hear the hymns of redemption that only daffodils can sing. I feel as small as I have ever felt.

My eyes grow large with the simple realization that when we make Lent about self-denial and self-sacrifice, it's still about self. When the only examination in which we engage is self-examination, the process creates isolation not engagement. When we focus on what is wrong, we can easily fail to be grateful for what is right.

I catch my breath. I think that perhaps I cannot wait until tonight to have the ashes smudged across my forehead, that perhaps I will this very moment run out into the branch, fall to my knees, plunge my hands into the black soot staining the ground, raise them to my face, and smear them across not just my forehead but also my cheeks, my chin, my nose, my carefully lined eyelids. I think that I must do something to demonstrate to this wide and wild and wonderful world that I am just happy to be here.

That is what I will do. That will be my Lenten observation. I will be happy to be here. I will, every day, be happy to be here, wherever here might be—a courtroom, an office, a front porch, a dirt road. Alone or in company. Harried or composed. I will be happy. And I will let the world know it.

I release my breath. I rise from the chair. I gather my purse, my car keys, my sunglasses. I walk out into the morning where the gentlest of breezes stirs up the remains of yesterday's fires and sends tiny wisps of ash floating out into the sky.

March 11, 2012

Somebody said that if I went outside around nine o'clock and looked in the western sky I could see Jupiter and Venus. So I went outside and stood in the middle of the big empty yard and stared at the place where I'm usually watching the sun sink. There they were, two white lights too big to be stars and too still to be airplanes, so they must be planets. I didn't see any rings around either of them—not that I expected to at that distance, of course—but it occurred to me at that moment that I was putting a lot of faith in what somebody else said, someone who might not know any more about this than I did.

The planetary fascination wore off pretty quickly and I had turned to go back inside when my attention was seized by the light in the sky on the other side of the yard—the moon, about half a wink away from full. Smudged a little by thin cloud cover, its relative nearness made it appear much larger than the planets at my back. What I know about the moon is no more certain than what I know about Jupiter and Venus. Men have been there, have walked on it, planted flags on it, and offered benedictory words over it, but I haven't. Yet, when I look at the moon, I feel entitled to use a possessive pronoun while leaving the planets with a definite article. Why?

There was a party at Sandhill last weekend. A celebration of the attaining of a dream. It was supposed to be an outdoor party and I planned outdoor decorations. Much-needed rain detoured those plans and everything got moved indoors, everything except a sign that my friend Lea helped me make. It's a mileage sign like the one that stood in the center of the 4077th M*A*S*H*, and it lists places beyond Sandhill that bear some significance to my life, that were the location of important events, that hold special memories.

When I finally stopped staring at the moon, my moon, and started back inside, my eyes fell on that sign, stuck in ground at the corner of the porch right at the base of a holly tree. The porch light reflected off the white letters like the sun reflects off the moon, and as I read the words I inserted the implied possessive pronoun before each one: my Saint Simons Island...my Wesleyan...my Ireland. And in doing so, I answered my question.

Why is it my moon, but not my Jupiter or my Venus? It is, as Antoine de Saint-Exupery's Fox explains to the Little Prince, about being tamed. Through long association, though not necessarily the intent to do so, the moon and I have become connected. Through long association and appreciation we have come to know each other as only the best of friends can. When I stare at it, I do so not with fascination but with longing, sometimes even wistfulness.

But it is not just the moon that I have tamed with my attention and with my affection. I have tamed Saint Simons and Sandhill and all the other spots on the map where my heart finds rest. I have tamed all the people who drove through rain and maneuvered through mud to gather for the celebration of the dream. I have tamed the words that find their way to the page, then out into the world.

It is because I have tamed them and because they have tamed me that they are my moon, my people, my words. And what I, what none of us must ever forget, is that as the Fox reminds the Little Prince, "You become responsible forever for what you have tamed."

March 25, 2012

The sun did not rise today. It sprang. Did not slowly inch into the sky. Catapulted. Went from being a clean, sharp, compass-drawn arc behind the tree line to a barely round blotch midway up the sky, its lower half covered by a cloud like a towel wrapped around its waist. A towel made of long-staple Egyptian cotton. Extra thick. Talcum-powder soft.

I wanted to touch it. I wanted to reach through the

windshield, through the early spring morning, through the light that left the sun 93 million light years ago, and touch that towel, run my fingers through the pile, feel it tickle the thin skin on the backs of my hands. I wanted to hold that towel up to my face and feel the just-out-of-the-dryer warmth on my cheeks, let my eyelashes catch on the loops like Velcro. I wanted to wrap my whole self up in that towel like a caterpillar inside a leaf.

But I remember my Greek mythology. Icarus flying too close. Phaethon driving too close. The moral of those stories? The sun must not be touched. A respectful distance must be kept. And so I pulled back my hand, curled it into a firm grip on the steering wheel, and steered my chariot north, away from the heat.

We are, all of us, good at that. Equating a desire for beauty with danger and putting up barriers to prevent ourselves from getting too close. Asserting a need for personal space and justifying the behavior that allows the actual need for human connection to go unmet. Resisting the urge toward relationship out of fear that our reach will be met with empty air.

We are good, really good, at not touching.

Most of the time. But not all the time.

Just the other day I was visiting at a friend's house, sitting on a stool at the kitchen counter, when another guest, someone I know but not well, reached into the hair on the crown of my head and began playing with it—fisting a handful and then letting go three or four times. I didn't even turn around. Curly hair, I've learned, is like pregnancy. They both invite touch. Not just intimates, but near strangers, feel comfortable in reaching out to stroke the taut round belly of an expectant mother or the tight ringlets on someone else's head.

Almost as though caught in an irresistible magnetic pull exerted on the digits, the hand rises and gently falls into a pat, a rub, a grasp and fluff. The guarding of one's personal space and the reciprocal acknowledgment of another's is suspended just long enough to make contact, to reassure the one reaching that, yes, the curiosity is real.

Though we generally tend to trust the sense of sight over the others, preferring eyewitnesses to any other kind, honesty requires that we all admit to having been fooled by a mirage or two. There is a reason that we greet returning heroes, long-absent lovers, and newborn babies not just with adoring glances but also with hugs and kisses. Touch proves the reality, spans the chasm, eliminates the distance.

Somewhere along the road between Oliver and Egypt, on that stretch where the pine trees grow like the pickets in a very tall fence, I stopped thinking about touching the sun. At just about the same time, the morning light suddenly began pulsing through the trees like a strobe and falling on my arms—the sun touching me. Wrapping me up in a big, warm towel. Extra thick. Talcum-powder soft.

April 8, 2012

The sawtooth oaks in the backyard, the ones that started out as knee-high, pinky-sized saplings, tower over me now. They move in the breeze like crinolined ball gowns, all hip-swaying, bodice-gripping green chiffon. Their widest branches reach out curving, almost touching, debutantes holding hands before their names are called. They look like Scarlett O'Hara at the barbeque, all insolent and saucy, dangerously aware of their beauty and its seductive power. And, because there are two, the Tarleton twins don't have to fight. There is plenty to go around.

They are not inconspicuous. I notice them every day. In the morning as I leave, in the evening as I return. In sunrise light the dewdrops on their leaves are sequins. In the gloaming the dew is gone and the leaves' thin veins are embroidery on smooth velvet. Bookends. A matched set.

Except, of course, they are not matched. If you look

closely, take a peek up under the skirts of green leaves, you will see that one trunk is straight and true and its branches radiate out like bicycle spokes in orderly tiers. The other trunk is actually two conjoined trunks, one doing its best to grow straight and true and one growing away at a 45-degree angle as though afraid it might get cooties from unwanted contact.

The result is that the aberrant trunk and its branches monopolize one entire side of the tree. If I saw it off—an act I have contemplated more than once—the tree will be, if not ugly, at least not as beautiful as before. Misshapen and bald on one side. More Suellen or Carreen than Scarlett.

Perhaps, in time, new branches will grow from the remaining trunk. Perhaps, in time, the emptiness will be filled, the saw-scar healed, the severed trunk forgotten.

But there is also the possibility that the trunks cannot survive without each other. That the trunk with good posture, excellent dancing skills, and natural flirtation abilities needs the off-center trunk for something essential. Like balance.

Thus I have been living with, observing, and contemplating the sawtooth oaks. To trim or not to trim, that is the question.

And now it is Easter. Or very nearly. I get out of the car but stop on my way inside, still weighted down with purse and gym bag and the day's detritus, to absorb the sensory bombardment. A line of bright red lilies stands straight as the Royal British Guards. The verbena at the corner of the deck is a broad swipe of brilliant purple, pouring over the edges of its bed like a waterfall. The basil and mint and thyme, the parsley and sage and cilantro are filling their pots and the air. The chinaberry tree's pale lavender blooms mingle with the golden berries from autumn that, in the mild winter, have refused to fall.

I try to ignore the oak trees—the one so perfect in shape it could be a tree stencil and the other with its extra off-kilter trunk. I try not to look their way and be drawn back to my dilemma. I am unsuccessful. The breeze that has set the wind chime to singing has set the trees to dancing, and from the corner of my eye I can see them—swaying and waving, bouncing and bobbing, nodding at each other.

And in that moment I know.

My friend Lynn loves to watch *Dancing with the Stars*. She is mesmerized by the intricately choreographed movements of the quickstep and the foxtrot, the bold athleticism of the mambo, the gracefulness of the waltz. And she loves the shiny, sparkly, spangly costumes, especially the shoes.

But she knows that shine and sparkle and spangle are not required. And so she dances at every opportunity. In flip-flops and bedroom shoes. In bare feet. In a bathrobe. With other people, with her cat, alone. She dances because dance is what we Easter-celebrants call "an outward manifestation of an inward grace."

I set down the purse, the gym bag, the burden. There is no perfect tree and imperfect tree. There is only tree. There is no part and whole. There is only holy.

Not to trim, that is the answer.

April 22, 2012

On Sunday afternoon, while the sun turned my arms a sweet shade of spring pink, I crawled around on the deck nailing nails. Not new ones. Old ones. The original nails that turned two-by-fours and four-by-fours and whatevers-by-whatevers into the structure on which I now grow herbs and watch hummingbirds and read books and, once every twenty-eight days, walk outside to make sure the moon is compass-drawn round.

I was nailing the old nails because by some process that probably has a name given it by a mechanical engineer, but which reminds me of that plastic plug in the Thanksgiving turkey that pops up when the temperature inside is just right, the nails over time start rising from their flush position in the wood to a perpendicular stance that, ignored, causes great pain in the bottom of a bare foot. I was nailing the old nails because things need to be maintained. I was nailing the old nails because nobody else was going to.

So there I was, as I said, crawling around hammering in what I hoped was a logical sequence so that I wouldn't miss any of the recalcitrant nails, listening to the new wind chime hanging from the eaves outside the bedroom door, and thinking about the quote attributed to Mark Twain, "When the only tool you have is a hammer, everything looks like a nail."

The hammer with which I was clobbering the pop-up nails is not the only tool I have. I have screwdrivers—flathead and Phillips. I have pliers, a hand saw, a level, a retractable tape measure, and a cordless drill. I have duct tape, electrical tape, and blue painter's tape. In the bottom of my toolbox are any number of small plastic canisters containing screws and nuts and bolts of varying sizes. If the job had called for something else, then I would most likely have been prepared.

But because the short and spiky pieces of metal protruding up through the floor of my deck were, in fact, nails and not merely something that looked like nails, a hammer was what I needed. It's just that after about ten minutes I realized that the hammer which is perfectly suited to tapping short, thin picture-hanging nails into Sheetrock might not be up to the task of pounding back into the deck what were by then beginning to look like railroad spikes.

And it might have been about that time when I remembered that not long before, someone who shall remain nameless, but who has a Y chromosome, described mine as "not much of a hammer." At which point, said nameless Y-chromosome-carrying human produced a much larger version of a hammer and proceeded to prove his point by ripping apart, in less than a minute, an old wooden packing crate that I wanted to use to build something else.

Show-off.

I probably did need a bigger hammer. But I didn't have a bigger hammer. And if I went to borrow a bigger hammer, chances were that there would be an offer to do the nailing for me. And I wanted to do it myself.

I can be stubborn.

So I kept at it. One, two, three, sometimes four blows to send one nail back down through a channel that had already been cut. Four swings to level a nail that was offering little or no resistance. Four licks to accomplish what could have been done with one. I switched from my right hand to my left and back again. I got tired.

I can be foolish, too.

Not every challenge can be met with perfect efficiency. Sometimes you have to use a tailgate as a stepladder, tack up a hem with masking tape, prop the door with a brick. Sometimes you have to make do. But sometimes, maybe even most of the time, you don't.

I hit the last lick, stood up, and looked around at the once again barefoot-safe deck. I was glad to be finished, glad to have done it all myself, and glad to know that before it needed to be done again I was going to have a bigger hammer.

May 6, 2012

A couple of weeks ago I stopped for the mail and, before I could get my hand into the box, heard the distinct sounds of baby birds. I quickly drew back, suspecting that I might be in the crosshairs of the mama somewhere close by. A few seconds passed without the appearance of an angry female of the avian variety, and I reached back in, this time seeing two baby birds sprawled across the stack of sale papers and catalogs.

They were scrawny and ugly. All thin skin and sharp

angles, bulbous eyes and over-sized beaks. Still slick and gooey with the contents of their former eggs. They couldn't have been out of their eggs more than an hour or so by my guess, and their high-pitched squeaks and squawks conveyed a desperation that I interpreted as a call to action.

The nest filled the entire back wall of the mailbox, deep enough that an opening of only about four inches at the top allowed access. It would not be an easy chore to return the birds to the spot from which it was fairly obvious they had fallen, but I couldn't just walk off with my most recent invitation to save money on car insurance, the Going Places magazine from AAA, and a slightly-soiled Penny Saver assuming that they would resolve the dilemma by themselves.

I rolled the magazine into a half-pipe and slid it along the bottom of the mailbox, attempting to scoop up one of the babies. The angle from which I was working and the bird's determined refusal to cooperate did not, at first, result in success. It took three or four tries before I managed to get enough of the tiny little thing hanging on to the slightly splayed edges of the magazine to lift it and push it toward the nest.

The baby landed on the rim, promptly and wildly flinging his spastic wings forward so that he fell back on the spot from which I had so laboriously lifted him. I sighed. I may have made a caustic remark or two.

I tried again. And again. Eventually, the baby bird and his/her brother/sister were both back in the nest, and I was imagining a dinner table conversation in which the mama bird would offer up a tasty worm or two while the young'uns recounted their adventure trying to leave the nest—the perfect setting for motherly admonitions about behaving oneself and not trying to grow up too fast.

The next day was Saturday. I went to check the mail. It hadn't been delivered yet, and the two birds were, once again, outside the nest on the bottom of the mailbox. This time, though, there was no squeaking or squawking. They weren't moving, but they seemed to be breathing. I stood and stared, hands fluttering like spastic baby bird wings, my thoughts running from past—"Should I have done something differently?"—to present—"Is there anything I can do now?"—and back again—"Did the mama abandon them because of something I did?"

Maybe they weren't supposed to be put back in the nest. Maybe that had been their moment to leave, to fly. Maybe I had retarded their growth by a day. Maybe the mama was watching even now to see if they would struggle to their skinny little feet, flap their diaphanous little wings and take off.

I decided to wait. I would walk away. I would leave them to their birdness. I would not interfere.

It was hard.

Later, after the mailman's car had slowed down in front of Sandhill and then taken off again, kicking up dust like newborn colt, I went back out. Mail, but no birds. Nary a sign.

I want to believe, I want really hard to believe, that they shook themselves out of their lethargy, girded their loins, and flew away from the mailbox into the perfect blue sky. I have no idea if that is what actually happened. There are other options, but I have chosen not to consider them.

I have also decided, I think, to clean out the mailbox. The nest that has been inside for at least seven years can't possibly be the best place to lay eggs anymore. There must be mites and Lord knows what else in there. There's really not enough room for an adult bird to comfortably get in and out, what with the accretion of twigs and leaves and thread by each year's subsequent tenant. And, to be honest, despite my optimism, I'm not ready for the possibility of the need for another rescue attempt any time soon.

After a long time of living, I'm finally figuring out that, while I know I can't save everything, I'm always going to want to try, and sometimes it's better to remove the temptation.

May 20, 2012

I step out onto the deck and take a deep breath. The breeze, brisk but mild, brings no scent of flower or bough, but only the sound of the wind chimes dangling and dancing in the white light of morning. The wet towels I have shaken out into limp flags are draped over the railings of the deck, and by noon they will be dry and sun-rough.

It has been a busy few weeks. A schedule full of good things, good times, people I love. But I am tired. I am, like Martha, careful and troubled about many things. I am glad for a Saturday on which no one is expecting me to be anywhere, to do anything.

The plan is to engage my body, not my mind—weed the perennials, dead-head the lilies, edge the ivy that threatens to overtake the corner of the carport. I smear a little sunscreen over my cheeks, stuff my hair into the new pink baseball cap, and pull the stained gardening gloves over fingernails that I suddenly realize are in serious need of attention.

That's when I notice it. The fairy path. Wending its way from under the low drooping branches of the sycamore tree across the backyard toward the cornfield, a clearly curving line of irregularly spaced and oddly shaped mushrooms. Several the size of large buttons, a couple as big as a demitasse cup. Three huddled together like matryoshka dolls.

According to the folklore of the Celtic peoples, fairy paths are routes taken by fairies between geographical sites of significance—fairy forts and mountains, streams, thorn bushes, ancient stone monuments—and must not be obstructed by human construction. If one's home is built on a fairy path, the doors and windows must be kept open at night to allow the fairies to pass through, and the consequences of not doing so are grave. Sometimes, it is said, a fairy path, which is usually invisible, can be identified by a strip of grass across a field that is a different color green from the rest. And sometimes, as in this case, the fairy path or a fairy ring (used for dancing) becomes visible by the appearance of mushrooms.

I am intrigued. No. That is not right. I am mesmerized. I stand so still and so quietly that I stop hearing the wind chimes, the rustle of leaves, the birds in the branch. But there are things to do. Perennials to be weeded. Lilies to be dead-headed. Ivy to be edged.

I shake my head to break the spell. Kneeling down, my back to the fairy path, I push my hands into the dense green screen that is periwinkle and coreopsis and Russian sage and begin pulling out errant sprigs of grass and clover. There are roots that hold tight to the earth and whose grips will have to be forced loose. I twist and wiggle, dig around the edges, twist and wiggle some more. In my haste I pull too soon and end up with a fist full of stem, the root still in the ground. I sigh with exasperation, rest back on my heels, straighten my tense shoulders.

Weeding, dead-heading, edging must wait.

I have to duck my head to stand under the lowest limbs of the sycamore tree, the spot where the fairy path begins. There is great danger, it is said, associated with traveling a fairy path when it might be in use by the fairies, but there is no danger here. I am quite sure that I have been invited, perhaps even summoned.

Feet together, arms at my side, I take a step and then another. Deliberate steps with pauses between. Careful steps so as not to touch the mushrooms. I follow the curve, realizing as I do that I am walking east toward the still rising sun, away from the shadow of the tree.

And then I am at the end. The point beyond which the path no longer shows me the way.

I stop. Breathe. Shift my stance from attention to parade rest. Realize that I am hearing the wind chimes again, their music joined this time by that of the temple bells hanging in the chinaberry tree. I close my eyes and lift my chin to feel the sun land on my face. Raise my arms, hold them there, suspended between heaven and earth, until my muscles burn and twitch.

When I open my eyes there has been no miraculous extension of the path. I've been given no revelation as to where I go from here. No magic decoder ring has been placed on my finger. But I am different. I am no longer tired. I am no longer troubled about many things. And the entire cornfield, not just one strip, is greener.

June 3, 2012

Basil, it is said, wards off dragons. I learned this long after I started growing basil in the big clay pot on the deck. Long after I mastered the technique the witty and beautiful people of the Food Network call "chiffonade" (the process of rolling the deep green leaves into tiny cigars and slicing them into slender ribbons of fragrance). Long after I decided that, when the time comes, I'd like my casket filled with fresh-cut basil so that I can leave this world surrounded by the scent of spring.

I learned it, in fact, only recently and cannot attest to the truth of the statement, but it does occur to me that whatever beasts of the dragon variety may live in the far reaches of the branch behind Sandhill have been held at bay to date.

I am a farmer's daughter. I know a little something about sowing and reaping. Seeds or plants go into the ground with the eye toward reproduction, multiplication, harvest of more than that with which you started. In a world of insecticides and fungicides and herbicides and outside the realm of organic farming, there's not a lot of planting for defensive purposes.

So the whole idea of this tiny little plant arresting the advance of a monster arouses my curiosity, and the thought that what we plant, what we grow, what we tend and nurture does more than produce but also prevents now has me wondering about the other green things I've stuck into the ground like stockade poles. I'm not necessarily concerned with whether the chinaberry tree, that source of my father's constant wonderment, has some part in forestalling the advance of ogres or whether the thyme and sage guard against trolls. I'm not even thinking about whether the azaleas, the hydrangeas, the hostas are anything more than decoration, sort of like the Queen's Guard outside Buckingham Palace—standing there and looking nice but not much of a defense against the wildness that, left untended, would overtake the yard in a matter of weeks.

I'm thinking of other lands, more exploitable and vulnerable lands. Miles and miles of what the old Westerns called the frontier, that which lies beyond a boundary, beyond what is known. The ground that is most susceptible to dragons and other hellish creatures is not that which creeps beneath my fingernails or blackens the bottoms of my bare feet. It is not surveyable, conveyable, devisable acreage. It is the interior real estate. The land of the heart, the soul.

There is a reason we call it a stream of thought. A field of study. A flood of emotions. The landscape within has its own topography. Rivers and creeks of memory and curiosity, pastures and deserts of interest and intellect, tides and currents of anger and sadness and love.

Often sightseen and visited, occasionally occupied or squatted upon, frequently over-logged or strip-mined, but only rarely, I think, is the heart, the soul, cleared for construction of a home, a place to stay. Too seldom do we, do I, unroll the plat and walk the lines, dig under the fallen leaves to find the rebar set at the corner so we know what is ours.

It is not impossible, however. Too seldom doesn't mean never. The terrain of one's heart can be learned like the farmer, the hunter, the hiker learns a piece of land—with intention and attention. With slowness of pace and undistracted vision. With time, lots and lots of time.

I went walking in the woods the other day, scooting

carefully down the hill from the path over the pond dam into a circus tent of bright green leaves. It had been a long time since I'd given myself over to purposeless roaming, and it felt good to be surrounded by nothing but tall trunks and slender branches. I did not pay attention to where I was going. I didn't have to. I have spent hours walking these woods. I know them. I know what grows here.

I believe I know the countryside of my heart and mind just that well. I believe I know what grows there. And, just in case there are dragons, I've planted basil.

June 17, 2012

With all the rain we've gotten lately, from Tropical Storm Beryl and various other low-pressure systems, the corn may well be as high as an elephant's eye. My memories of the Grant Park Zoo, formed when I was considerably shorter than I am now, leave me a little vague as to how high that is exactly, but it is safe to assume, I think, higher than my head, and the corn is definitely that.

When we were children, Keith, Aunt June, and I used to run through the cornfield chasing each other and playing "Bonanza" while Mama, Daddy, and Grannie broke the ears that would be cut and scraped and bagged and put into the freezer so that on every Sunday table for the coming year there would be a bowl of sweet creamy summer. We ran through rows that still held the warmth of late afternoon sun, tattooing our bare feet with stone bruises and tagging our arms and legs with the graffiti of bright red blood, tiny cuts sliced by the razor edge of corn fronds.

Stray hairs decoupaged with sweat against our foreheads, we did not stop until dark, until our parents' arms, buckets, car trunks were full of heavy green ears and we could rush inside, past the swarm of bugs dive-bombing the porch light, and fall on the floor in front of the window-unit air conditioner. We stayed there, cotton shirts stuck to our backs, the salt in our sweat making tiny white clouds appear on the fabric as it dried, until Mama appeared with glasses of Kool-Aid, red like the jagged lines on our legs, in glasses dripping with condensation all the way across the kitchen floor.

Some afternoons Daddy would walk outside to the edge of the field and break three or four ears on his way in from work. He would shuck them, strip away the ribbed husks and silky tassels, crack off the hard stems on the end with a quick snap, and toss them under the broiler for a few minutes to roast. The kernels turned brown and chewy like caramel and we would sit on the front steps to eat them, hands grasping either end of the cobs, elbows propped on knees to eliminate all unnecessary motion as we gnawed our way from one end to the other of this first, blessed offering of the season.

There were no questions then. No uncertainties. No mistrust of anything in my world, the one that was triangulated by home and school and church. The one populated by people whose stories I knew, whose names were among the first words I learned, whose faces still materialize when I smell honeysuckle or stoop to pick verbena or taste homemade lemonade.

Wistfulness moves through my body like a sudden chill. I am sitting on the deck, staring across the yard—not 25 feet—at the cornfield that rises like a green curtain, glowing with the sheen of a full-detail wax job. Straight as a plumb line the stalks stand in endless rows that stretch from here to there. From here to beyond there. From here to somewhere else. The tassels are pale gold and bobbing like a jester's cap, a windsock of sorts. The ears are jutting out at just the right angle, three to a stalk, medals pinned to the chests of soldiers at attention.

It could be the same field through which I ran wildly forty-five years ago, slapping my thigh as though it were the flanks of a stallion, chasing Indians across the flat acres of the Ponderosa. But it is not the same field. I am not the freckled ten-year-old. My fatigue cannot be assuaged by a glass of Kool-Aid.

I realize that I am halfway listening for the voice of James Earl Jones to come rolling out of the branch, the stalks to part and Shoeless Joe Jackson to walk into the yard. I am looking for salvation from a world beyond this one because—having left undone those things which I ought to have done and done those things which I ought not to have done far too often lately—I am too tired, too spent, too frustrated to save myself.

There is, of course, no voice, no appearance, but I keep staring into the shimmering emerald shadows and, as I do, I feel my breath slowing, slowing to take in the sweet green scent of corn, which tickles me somehow. I laugh. At the memories, at my *Field of Dreams* imaginings, at the preposterous idea that I could, tired or frustrated or at my very best, ever save myself.

And suddenly, I recognize where I am. Not just at the edge of a cornfield, but at Point A of a brand new triangulation, a rebar set, a monument laid, an altar where I can offer up a prayer of gratitude for all the stories I don't yet know.

July 1, 2012

This week my friend Lea found herself packing up and leaving forever a place that she dearly loves. It has belonged to her family for over forty years and has held not just the funky, eclectic mixture of furniture that houses at the beach normally collect but also significant memories for four generations and more than a little piece of each of their hearts. Her last night there, it was just Lea and a blow-up mattress and two lawn chairs. She wrote on her Facebook wall, "Feeling like Sam in the last episode of Cheers where he is the last person left, takes one last look around, then turns out the light, walks out and closes the door behind him."

The next day she sent her friends an e-mail listing all the items that had been crammed into her car in the hours before vacating the premises. It was a long and impressive list and included, among things one would expect like clothes and work items, "five brooms …two rolls of toilet paper…1 plastic box of paintbrushes, 1 large plastic tub of craft paints, 3 large plastic shopping bags of craft supplies…1 big box of things I need in my car (sharpies, paper, tape, koosies, etc)…1 big metal tin of books and stuff I keep in my car always…1 iron to give away."

One of her friends replied, "That is going to be a mess on the road if you have an accident." All I could think was, "Lord, have mercy!"

It would be a mess if Lea's car, like a defective pressure cooker, spontaneously erupted somewhere on Highway 17, spewing brooms and paintbrushes and small appliances all over the right-of-way. It would have been a bigger mess, however, had she not loaded that car, had she not taken one last look around, turned out the light, and closed the door behind her because this is what I have observed:

There is a point in every growing season at which the growing medium—field, garden, plot, pot —becomes messy. The rows lose their delineation, the individual plants lose their edges, and it becomes impossible to identify any point as the beginning or the end. It is in that moment that the farmer/gardener/tender of soil loses control of the structure, the aesthetics, and the end result.

Example: The cornfield outside my window is now beyond plowable, its edges crowded by a jumble of knee-high grasses and weeds and its canopy of wide green fronds woven together in uneven bands, like the warp and weft of the potholders I used to make on a little red metal loom. Another example: The verbena at the corner of the house that started out as six little identical plants has morphed into wild and spindly vines spread over the ground like fingerpaint—

randomly, awkwardly, all over each other and the stone edgers meant to contain them.

I don't like messy. I like neat and tidy. I like order and organization and anything alphabetized, and so it has taken some time for me to learn that messiness cannot be avoided if one wants to grow. Plant a seed and dirt will make its way under your fingernails, despite the gardening gloves. Write a story and the first draft will end up in a wadded paper ball on the floor. Open your heart and take the risk that, like Lea's car, a bump in the road or a crash into someone else could send everything inside flying out into the open sky.

It has taken time to learn those things, but I have learned them. I have learned them by planting the seed, writing the story, opening my heart, and, consequently, scrubbing my fingernails, picking up the endless mounds of paper balls, and standing on the side of the road watching the wind from speeding traffic carelessly toss about that which I hold most precious.

The result is that I have grown. And I am still growing. And the messiness of that is something to embrace.

July 15, 2012

I am, I've been told, a good storyteller. I've been told this enough that I've come to accept it as true.

One should be careful about what one accepts as true.

Last week I took off a couple of days to spend time at the beach with friends. One night a number of us gathered at a local barbecue place for supper, sat outside at a long weathered picnic table, let the wood smoke settle into our clothes and hair, and forgot about the world on the other end of the causeway. The food and atmosphere were good, the conversation better.

When we'd finished off the barbecue and potato salad and fried Oreos, our bodies tired from a long day in the sun and our brains just about empty of things like deadlines and to-do lists, we adjourned from the barbecue joint and reconvened a few blocks away at my friends' family beach house. The collection of four girls had ice cream cones and chased the dog around the backyard and then came inside just about the time the grown-ups sat down to continue the conversations that, somehow, you just never get around to having at home.

And that's when the stories started. Something reminded somebody of something and we laughed, and that reminded me of something else and I said, "Remember when?" and, the next thing I knew, Katie Anne, the youngest of the four assorted girls, was on the arm of my chair, her face locked on mine, mimicking my expressions, smiling and scowling at all the right moments, laughing on cue.

"Tell us another story," she said. And I gladly did.

Eventually it was time to break up the party, but I promised Katie Anne that I had more stories, one really good story, in fact, and that I would share it the next day at the pool where we'd all agreed we would see each other again.

I looked forward to telling Katie Anne the story. It's a good story. Everybody I've ever told this story liked it. Katie Anne would like it, too. I was sure of it.

I shouldn't have been.

The next day, as the other girls squealed and splashed in the pool, chased each other and the sole boy cousin who had come along, Katie Anne sat at the end of the lounge chair where I had spread out an appropriately garish beach towel and listened to the story. Except this time her face didn't stay locked on mine, she didn't mimic my expression, she scowled a good bit more than she smiled, and she—most obviously—did not laugh.

When I got to the end, she stood up and walked over to the ladder at the deep end of the pool. "So, Katie Anne, did you like the story?" I called.

"It was long," she offered and jumped into the water.

I and her mother, who was sitting nearby, now did the laughing. So much for being a good storyteller.

She was right though. The story was long. And long is not what Katie Anne had wanted, expected, or needed when a pool full of children was right there within reach. Life can be like that. When what you get isn't what you want, expect, or need it can seem nothing short of long.

Notice, though, that Katie Anne didn't say the story was *too* long. She didn't offer that it was longer than necessary, desirable, or right. It was simply long. And it is in that differentiation that I found the real point of her declaration.

Life—in its entirety or on any given day—isn't *too* anything. It simply is. Long or short. Exhilarating or exhausting. Confusing or enlightening. The same goes for one's work, relationships, dreams. None of them is more than or less than necessary, desirable, or right. Attaching adverbs like *too* and *very* and *overly* to people and experiences is disrespectful at best and dangerous at worst. We steal from ourselves when we choose to do so.

My story was long. Just long. I'm still a good storyteller and I will tell that story again. Just not to Katie Anne.

July 29, 2012

Tonight at about eight o'clock I went outside to get a closer look at a fawn that was nibbling away at Daddy's peanuts in the field on the west side of the house. He'd been there earlier in the day when a couple of friends were visiting, but a passing car spooked him. In the late afternoon sun he'd ventured back out for another meal of the smooth green leaves and tiny yellow blooms folded flat like cut-out paper Valentines. I moved slowly down the field road with my camera in hopes that when he noticed me and took off running for cover I would be able to get a video for my friends.

He did eventually notice me and I did get a little footage

of his tiny white tail bouncing across the field. When he disappeared from view, I realized that I had tracked him into the middle of the field, that there were long straight lines stretching out on either side of me, and that the sandy white paths running between the rows reminded me of a labyrinth. Kind of.

I walked down the full length of one row, counted over ten rows—a random number that seemed just the right width—and turned back into the field in the opposite direction. At the end of that row, I counted over another ten rows and began again. Up, over, down, over. Up, over, down, over.

No one can be sure, but it is thought that the first labyrinths, built thousands of years ago, were meant to symbolize the paths to be followed in life, in daily and seasonal cycles, from birth to death to rebirth, and to mimic the path of the sun in its circuit across the sky. Later, they were adopted by Christians as a substitute for long pilgrimages and symbolized the long and difficult path that the Christian followed toward redemption.

A true labyrinth contains no tricks or deceptions, no dead ends. It is a single wandering path that leads from an entrance to the center and back again.

At first I strolled slowly, hands clasped behind me, and I could almost see myself in a loose brown robe, barefoot, hair springing out in all directions, the reverential abbess of The Abbey of Sandhill. The venerable vision didn't last long, however. My natural stride, long and quick and purposeful, took over and it was just me moving up and down, back and forth.

I didn't move so quickly, though, that I missed the signs of life at my feet—the divots of dirt left by the deep treads of marauding deer, the patches of grass sprouting up through the peanut vines, the wide tractor tire tracks. Across the way the sun was setting, warming the horizon with a low flame. The heat of the day was lifting and drawing with it into the fading sky the distant sounds of dogs barking, four-wheelers revving, my own thoughts almost audible.

I figure I'd walked about a mile, weaving back and forth, by the time the flame went out over the treetops. And, just as with a real labyrinth, I came out where I started. So what, then, is the point? Isn't a pilgrimage about getting somewhere? About making progress?

In Greek mythology Theseus went to the center of the labyrinth in order to slay the Minotaur, the monster inside. There is, of course, a monster inside each of us. The monster of selfishness, of insensitivity, of pride and greed and envy. The monster will not slay itself and it will not come out on its own. We, each of us, must walk the narrow path to the center of our selves, face down and destroy the monster, and find our way back out. Out to the place of beginning.

In a few weeks the peanut vines will be lapped over, the rows hard to distinguish, the field one broad swath of dark green. Beneath it will be footprints finding their way to the center and back.

August 12, 2012

In opening the back door, I flush a flock of birds at the edge of the branch, their wings fluttering fast and thick like shuffled cards. They rise and disappear too quickly for me to make out any markings and they make no sound from which I, were I a person who knew birdcalls, could identify them. The strip of field grass, broom sedge, and dandelions that separates the branch from the backyard is relatively narrow and, on this filmy, overcast morning, the birds' small feathered bodies are little more than momentary smudges across my contact lenses.

Two or three times a year Daddy or my brother Keith, swinging the rotary cutter around the edges of the adjacent fields, will turn wide to include my little strip, but most of the time it remains as it is now—knee-high in something, soft and crunchy underfoot.

A few weeks ago some friends and I visited Little St. Simons Island, one of those "I've always wanted to go there, can't believe I've never been there" places. Accessible only by boat, it was formed from the sediment of the Altamaha River and has doubled in size since the first survey was made in the 1860s. In the last four years alone, it has gained 30 feet of shoreline.

Bouncing around in the bed of a white Chevy pickup, we ducked to avoid the branches of live oaks and Southern red cedars, pines and palmettoes, a canopy of trees that has never been harvested. We saw a black-necked stilt, who has the longest legs per body length of any bird, and a roseate spoonbill, two of the 283 species of birds that live among the 10,000 acres, and a fallow deer, descendant of the first ones brought to the island from a zoo in New York in exchange for alligators.

The heat was bad, the gnats and mosquitoes worse, but I was so overwhelmed by all that I did not know, had never seen, wanted so desperately to remember that neither the heat nor the pests were much of a bother. And in the midst of the sensory onslaught, I learned a new word: ecotone.

Words are playthings. They are tools. They are tastes and textures and smells. And a new one is a gift wrapped in tissue paper and tied up with wide satin ribbon.

An ecotone is a transition area between two different patches of landscape, a habitat particularly significant for mobile animals because it allows them to exploit more than one set of habitats. The barrier islands of Georgia are an ecotone—anteroom for entering the mainland from the ocean, foyer to the ocean from the mainland. Marsh and reed bed and wetlands, all forming a bridge between worlds. So is, I realized as the unidentified birds flitted away from my noisiness into the dimness of the branch, my narrow isthmus of land, my band of untamed, unmown grass and bush and weed.

It seems fairly obvious that the concept of ecotone doesn't need to be limited to topography. Landscape exists within a personality or a lifespan. It can be found within a relationship or a conversation or a performance. It is that place or moment when movement becomes obvious, when change has to be acknowledged, when the next thing is no longer frightening or strenuous or disagreeable, but simply the next thing.

And it is equally apparent that the ecotone, at least in the non-topographical sense, is a temporary locale. It is not a place for abiding, but sojourning. A place for catching one's breath, perhaps. For taking a last look in either direction before setting out for good.

I see that now. I realize that it is time to move. Time to explore another habitat. Time to see more of those "always wanted to go there, can't believe I've never been there" places in the world and in my heart.

All is silent. The evaporation of the birds into the mist has left the morning gray and green and still. I untie the ribbon, unfold the paper, and toss the brand new word into the warm summer air.

August 26, 2012

On one side is a field of cotton. The stems are blooming with pink and white flowers, soft and sweet like appliques on a gingham sundress. On the other side is a field of corn. The stalks are stiff, the fronds brittle, the ears hard as a brick bat. What was pulsing, quivering green is now lethargic tan, the color of a cup of coffee gone cold. In between, in the middle, is the road.

That is where I am. The middle. Looking from side to side. Comparing and contrasting. Noting that this is an odd season, one in which some crops are made, ready for harvest, and others are on the cusp of what they are yet to become.

I want to sit there a while, listen to the voices of the cotton and the corn approach from either side and mingle over my head. There is something in the middle that wants to be heard.

I drive on.

Occasionally my nephew Adam e-mails me a YouTube video. It is usually a country music performer or a vituperative political commentator. Today it is Erk.

As an assistant coach at the University of Georgia, Erk Russell gave the moniker "Junkyard Dawgs" to Georgia's undersized defense and butted heads with his players to celebrate a good play. Leaving Athens to restart a football program at Georgia Southern where the sport hadn't been played for forty years, he proceeded to lead the team to three national championships. He was football royalty. He was also my friend. He loved a good lawyer joke and never spared my feelings when telling one. He loved words as well, and occasionally I would get a note in cursive too beautiful to be written by a man telling me he'd particularly enjoyed my column that week.

I double-click on the video and lean back to watch. It is an interview conducted during the 1987 playoffs. It is vintage Erk. He explains Beautiful Eagle Creek and gives a plug for Snooky's and tells the rattlesnake story. I listen like I listen to hymns in church, with half an ear because I know them so well. The Alabama drawl that never left him and could be exaggerated at will make him sound like he is standing in the doorway.

The voiceover cuts in to mention that Erk was fifty-five when he came to Statesboro. The number startles me. Fifty-five. That's how old I am.

I finish watching the video and send Adam a response: "You were five years old. You grew up going to those games and watching him coach and you didn't even know what you were seeing. He was fifty-five when he came to Georgia

Southern and the work for which we remember him most he did after that. Kinda makes me think I might have a little something left in me."

I hit "send," hoping he will laugh, hoping that maybe this nephew to whom I have always been a grown-up will respond with something along the lines of, "Don't be silly, Kap. There's a lot left in you."

He does not.

I get back to work. I make telephone calls, answer telephone calls, draft petitions. And all the while the corn and the cotton are humming in the background.

On the way home I stop to visit with a friend. Conversation turns to a book she is reading, which I have already read. It is titled *Notes on a Mid-Faith Crisis* and includes a chapter called "Middle Voice." There are a few languages, the author points out, including ancient Greek, that have, in addition to the active and passive voices, what is called the middle voice. It is used to indicate situations in which the subject of the sentence is changed by the action of the verb but not just passively acted upon, when the subject is at least partially responsible for what has happened. "When you are somewhere," she writes, "between the agent and the one acted upon. When you have something done to you. *I will have myself carried. I will have myself saved.*"

My friend, who is almost my age and asking herself a lot of questions these days, has just read this chapter. "I think," she says, "that maybe I am in the middle." There is something in her words that sounds exactly right, so I nod in agreement, but it is only later that I realize they are also revolutionary.

Middle voice has little use in a society in which self-reliance is the religion of choice, in which pop culture deifies defiance, and in which daily doses of doomsday prophecy eviscerate even the hardiest of souls. And yet there is such a need for it. A need to deliberately choose to be less than deliberate, to purposefully yield to the current, to intentionally sail with rather than against the tide.

I will not be fifty-five much longer. Another birthday breaks the horizon. There are things that are finished. There are things that will not be done. But sitting in the road between the cotton and the corn I think that, perhaps, I may have finally come to the place where I will have myself carried. The season between the blooming and the dying will have itself lived.

September 9, 2012

My very first class at Wesleyan was Survey of American Literature taught by Dr. Leah Strong. The class met in Tate Hall at the end of the second floor overlooking the library. The ceilings were tall, the walls plaster, and the dark wooden windows so heavy that when they were opened, which was fairly often because there was no air-conditioning in Tate at that time, you could hear the chains creaking in the sashes halfway across campus. It was a beautiful Indian summer day and the sunshine seemed to move in waves with the breeze that ruffled the gingko leaves. My classmates and I, probably ten or twelve or us, were sitting in old wooden desks whose tops had been scarred with fifty years of initials and class names carved by the pens and pencils of daydreaming Wesleyannes.

I was sitting there wondering just how long one was supposed to wait for a professor when a figure came scurrying through the doorway. It was a short, chubby gray-haired woman wearing grannie glasses, black polyester pants, a Hawaiian print shirt, and shoes my father would call brogans. She was carrying under her arm, not a briefcase or a textbook or a sheaf of lecture notes, but a motorcycle helmet.

She strode determinedly across the front of the room, set her helmet down in the middle of the desk, and then walked around to the front and jumped backward onto the desk, leaving her short legs dangling like those of a marionette.

She looked around the room at us and said, "The definition of poetry . . . ." We hurriedly opened our brand new spiral notebooks and poised our pens over the clean white page.

"The definition of poetry . . . ." She looked around the room again. "When I was a child, my father used to bring home packages of paper pellets. These pellets were the size of BB's and when you dropped one of these pellets into a glass of water it would slowly begin to unfold and unfurl until, a few minutes later, the pellet had become a beautiful flower. Each of the pellets was different. Each one produced a uniquely beautiful flower."

She looked around the room a third time. "The poem is the pellet and you are the glass of water."

I realized I was staring. I had not written a single word. And all I could think was "Oh, my Lord, I'm going to love college."

With such an introduction, it would be understandable if Leah Strong did not live up to the expectations created that day. But she did. She introduced me to the ideas of popular culture and folklore and taught me that the stories my family told, the songs my family sang, the language my family used—MY family, strong and wise and unaffected country people—were things to be valued and preserved. She trained my ear to the cadence and melody of Southern voices, alerted me to the layered meanings of colloquialisms, made me tender to the weightiness of words like "home" and "place."

I did not know these things, of course, when I shook her hand for the last time before I left Wesleyan as a student. I did not know how to articulate them when I saw her years later at a reunion. It is too late to tell her now.

I was thinking about Dr. Strong today as I remembered a conversation I had over the weekend with my niece Kate and her mother Katherine. I'd just returned from a visit with an older friend who is losing some of her independence, and I couldn't find the words to express the feeling of choking grief that had me by the throat. I started crying.

"The whole cycle of life thing?" Katherine asked and I nodded.

Kate looked at me quizzically. "You're crying over photosynthesis?"

It is difficult to laugh and cry simultaneously. Hard to tell which one is causing you to lose your breath and which is making your stomach hurt. And this time, at least, it didn't matter.

Just like the poem as pellet, Kate had found the perfect metaphor. Or something like that. And in the warm September sun I could see Dr. Strong sitting on the edge of that desk, and she was smiling.

September 23, 2012

There are five of us around the table. The four children are seated; I am standing, walking from end to end, looking over their shoulders at their work. Strung along the center of the table are bottles of glue, pairs of scissors, and stacks of magazines. In front of each child is a single piece of white paper. The exercise I've given them in this class for young writers is to make a collage representing an object each of them has drawn from a bag. One of the girls has drawn a broken seashell, the other girl a ceramic miniature of an English country church. The two boys have drawn strangely contrasting items—an iron railroad spike and a makeup brush.

I am teaching this class for a lot of reasons, not the least of which is the fact that I love children, enjoy watching their faces as they struggle to grasp new concepts or think of the right word. They don't know how to mask their emotions or feel the need to equivocate. It is good to hear the truth from the mouth of someone who doesn't yet know that there is another option. One of them, when I asked what words they would use to describe me, said, "Old." There was a quizzical look on her face when I gasped in mock horror.

I am also teaching this class because I enjoy being a student and I know that, whatever I may teach these children about words and writing, they are sure to teach me at least as much about life.

There is a time limit and, with five minutes to go, I remind them that they need to start gluing their images to the paper. One of the girls, the youngest in the class, has discovered that each of the bottles has a stopper inside that must be removed before the creamy white glue can be squirted out of the bright orange twist-tops. I didn't know this. I've never seen such a thing. We pause a moment and discuss why the glue makers might have done this. Someone mentions something about getting glue on clothes. There is, obviously, a story behind the comment. Maybe that story will get written down.

Each of the bottles has now been liberated, but one of them, the one being used by the boy with the makeup brush, is still not flowing. It takes me a moment to realize what he is doing to address the dilemma: he has taken the big orange-handled scissors, gripped them in his fist by the shaft of the blades, and begun trying to jam the closed blades into the tiny hole in the glue top.

I burst out laughing. I can't help myself. They look at me as though I've lost my mind. I try to explain: "Look at you! You're a man! This is exactly what a man does! Something doesn't work and you grab the biggest tool you can find and start hitting on it!" I was about to lose my breath.

This child is ten years old. Cute as a button. Smart as a whip. (Did I mention we were working on similes?) He's got this impish smile that alerts you to the fact that he's up to something, even if it's only in his imagination, and makes you want to squeeze his cheeks—which you don't, of course. He is ten years old and still a little boy, and yet he's already approaching problems in a gender-specific (and maybe stereotypical) way.

I don't stop him. I stand close by and make sure he doesn't hurt himself, but I allow him to do it his way. He manages to unclog the glue bottle and finish his collage. And I finally stop laughing.

The irony of his choice of objects from the bag is not lost on me. This boy's boy pulled out a makeup brush, even had to ask me what it was, but he didn't complain, didn't ask if he could choose again, simply set about the task at hand. And when a problem arose, he tackled it head on.

He wants to be a writer, but after today it occurs to me that if writing doesn't work out, this boy would make a mighty fine Marine: "Improvise, adapt, and overcome."

October 7, 2012

I was about three years old. Mama and Daddy had left Keith and me with a babysitter. It was a most unusual event in light of two things. First, they rarely went anywhere that the two of us couldn't go as well, and if they did, there were any number of aunts and uncles with whom we could have stayed, eliminating the need for a babysitter. The other unusual element to the evening was where they went—to a gospel sing, a gathering of various gospel singers and quartets and maybe even a choir or two.

Mama loves gospel music. At any given moment on any given day, if someone were to walk in on her unexpectedly she would probably be found singing all four verses of a shaped-note hymn she'd learned as a girl. Particularly noteworthy was the fact that she had convinced Daddy to take her to the sing, an event separate and apart from a regular church service and also on a Saturday night.

It surprises me that I remember those background details from a time when I was a toddler, but I am as sure of them as I am of what happened while my parents were away.

I was sitting on the couch, vinyl embossed to resemble brocade. My legs stuck straight out in front of me, too short to bend over the edge of the seat. Across the room the blue-gray flickers of the television kept the apartment from being completely dark.

In my lap was a box of Sugar Pops, a rare treat in a home where breakfast involved grits and cubes of Triple-A margarine. I pushed my small fist through the cardboard flaps, grabbed a handful of cereal, and pulled it back out. I had developed a rhythm. Push in, pull out. I have no idea how many fistfuls of Sugar Pops I'd eaten when I suddenly I heard myself chanting, "K-A-T-H-Y." I paused and chanted again, "K-A-T-H-Y."

After the second or third time, Phyllis the babysitter stared directly at me with a startled look on her face. She realized that I had spelled my name. I had a realization, too: these sounds, whatever they might be called, these sounds that I did not realize were letters, were *me*. K-A-T-H-Y: when breathed in that particular way in that particular order, the hard and soft puffs of air represented my self.

I stopped. I didn't say anything else. I didn't look at Phyllis. She didn't say anything either. The blue-gray flickers continued. I probably put my fist back into the cereal box. I don't remember.

Obviously I had heard, at some point, my parents talking to each other, and something in the tone of voice, the sidelong glances, the use of a whisper in a household where whispers were rare had alerted me to the significance of sounds I did not understand. K, A, T, H, and Y. And now I had deciphered the code. I felt like Dorothy walking through the gates of the Emerald City, granted access to something about which I understood only one thing: It was grand.

I did not know the word "epiphany" at age three, but years later when I read Phyllis Tickle's definition ("that moment, that instant in which a clarity so brilliant as to be only divinely possible drops into human life and takes up permanent residence"), I was able to understand it at least in part, I think, because of what happened that night. That night, letters and the words they build became my personal possessions. Other people might use them, but they would always be mine.

I have told the story before, but it is only in the writing of it, the *writing* of it, that I realize something important: the first word I ever spelled, the first thing I gave back to the world as a writer was my name, was myself. That is a dangerous precedent. And it makes it hard sometimes to tell the stories. Hard to find the right words, to arrange them in an order that tells the truth and, at the same time, shields the innocent, dispenses kindness, and extends forgiveness.

What would be harder, though, is not to tell them at all.

October 21, 2012

When I was a girl, the only college football games on television on Saturday afternoon involved teams whose nicknames I did not understand (Sooners, Buckeyes) and whose players' names all seemed to have too few vowels. I had no connection to Oklahoma or Ohio, Nebraska or Notre Dame, and it took me a long time to realize that I watched not for the competition itself but for the broadcast. I watched so I could hear Keith Jackson.

I probably heard him call thousands of plays over the years, but there is one call—probably because it said less about football and more about life—that I will never forget. It was late in the game. The quarterback of the trailing team was having a bad outing. He'd been intercepted. His completion percentage was negligible. He sat on the sidelines looking like, as Keith would probably have said, a whipped pup.

Conversation in the broadcast booth turned to whether

the coach would, when his team got the ball back, put in another quarterback. The starter clearly didn't have his best stuff. The backup was pretty good. It would make a lot of sense. And maybe the backup could surprise the defense. Maybe there was a miracle waiting to happen.

The camera got a close-up of the head coach, dressed in a coat and tie, notes rolled up in his hand, yelling out instructions as the offense took the field. And there was the quarterback, the starter, the struggling starter, running out with them.

"Well," said Keith Jackson in that stentorian voice that never lost its Southern accent, "looks like the coach believes that you dance with the one what brung ya'."

I have no recollection of how the game ended, whether the quarterback crafted a storybook ending or walked away the goat. I remember only that with those few words, an expression that, surprisingly, I'd never heard before, Keith Jackson presented me with an axiom that over the years has become something like a koan, a paradox on which to meditate, a question with more than one answer, a story that in the telling and retelling draws me closer to intuitive truth.

On that day, that autumn Saturday so many years ago, I understood the story to be about loyalty. The coach put the starting quarterback in for the final set of downs because of a previously affirmed allegiance, a declared determination to perform certain acts in support of a common goal. The act may well have been less a demonstration of confidence than a dare to condemn. No matter what happened, no one could fault the coach for being loyal.

It is another autumn Saturday, and I am outside working in the yard. The car radio is tuned to the University of Georgia pre-game show and the volume is turned up loudly enough for me to hear it as I reset the concrete edgers around the hosta bed. One of the broadcasters mentions Keith Jackson, long retired to California and endless rounds of golf, and that mention sends my mind careening back to the unnamed coach and the quarterback with whom he chose to dance. For the first time in a long time the koan appears, its feet (iamb, anapest, molossus) skipping, then tromping, then running breathlessly through my thoughts, looping around and around until I am nearly breathless myself.

I am staring at the clouds. They are high and white, appliques fused to the pale blue baby's bib of the sky. It has been forty years since I so assuredly analyzed the coach and the quarterback, their relationship and the dynamics of the moment Keith Jackson memorialized with a quaint colloquialism. I have experienced my share of interceptions; my statistics have been less than stellar in any number of categories. And I understand now, in this moment of reexamining and retelling, that it was not simply loyalty that put the quarterback back on the field. It was trust.

Loyalty is strong, but it is often blind. Trust is its companion animal. It prevents loyalty from stepping out into traffic and alerts it to unexpected changes in the environment. Trust knows when to abandon calls for reason and disregard demands for explanation. Trust can see in the dark.

And when the game—or something more important—is on the line, trust is the ability to see in the dark that will determine who gets to dance.

November 4, 2012

Our ninth grade literature textbook included Stephen Vincent Benet's post-apocalyptic short story, "By the Waters of Babylon." The story follows a young boy, the son of a priest in a primitive society, as he journeys far beyond the borders his people have long honored. His long and dangerous quest takes him to the city of the gods, where he stumbles across the ruins of the great towers that once filled the city. Two of the rocks have words written on them, words he doesn't understand:

UBTREAS and ASHING.

I remember this part of the story particularly well, probably because Marcia Lanier quizzed and prodded and cajoled us so thoroughly on what we thought those two words might mean. Probably because the entire story turned on those two strange words. Probably because when we finally put it all together, we figured out that the words were really only parts of words, that the stones were fragments of landmarks in New York City—the United States Subtreasury building and a statute of George Washington—and that the story took place not in the distant primitive past but in a very possible not-so-distant future.

Just the other day I found myself remembering "By the Waters of Babylon" and wondering what a young priest or priestess who came tiptoeing through the wreckage of one of our cities might find. She might stub her toe on a large piece of signage on which was written "ART" and be led to think that the tower over which it had hung was once dedicated to truth and beauty. Or he might trip over an equally large section on which was written "ALM" and think perhaps that the place had been a temple where care was provided for the poor and ill. Both of them would be wrong.

Because, of course, both ART and ALM would be broken-off pieces of a Walmart sign.

Walmart, the store into which I walked two weeks before Halloween to find Christmas decorations already available for sale and realized two things. First, the date on which I have to stop going into Walmart until after Christmas (the actual December 25th Christmas) in order to avoid crowd-induced anxiety attacks and general ill temper has reached a record early date on the calendar. And, second, when the apocalypse does come most of the bodies will be found inside Walmart Supercenters under mounds of flat-screen televisions, cartons of 500-count LED Christmas lights, and Dora the Explorer pajamas.

Okay. Maybe mine is an extreme reaction. Maybe there are those who don't mind, who actually enjoy navigating a maze of aisles lined with plastic holly wreaths and Lady Stetson gift sets in search of candy corn. Perhaps there are people who are not disturbed by the odd juxtaposition of a jack-o-lantern with the Baby Jesus on the end-cap of the express lane. It is even possible that, living here among my own people, there are folks not overcome by the sense that can only be described as the heebie-jeebies when they are accosted by the voice of Bing Crosby crooning away about a white Christmas from behind a rack of Darth Vader masks.

Extreme reaction or not, I couldn't help wondering, when our end comes, if it is in the nature of a cataclysm, whether we will leave behind anything worth rummaging through, stumbling over. For the ones left behind or coming after, will they think we were dedicated to truth and beauty, that we provided for the poor and the ill? Or will the evidence of our existence leave them thinking, as the young boy in Benet's story thought, that we had lived in a place of great riches but squandered their magic?

I want to believe that somewhere, between the racks of Spiderman costumes and the shelves of scented candles, between the fun-size candy bars and the needlepoint stockings, behind the scarecrows and hay bales, under the blow-up snowmen, those great riches still exist. I think we can find them.

November 28, 2012

When I was a little girl, our vacations always sent us north toward Rock City and Ruby Falls, Stone Mountain and Grant Park, Cherokee and the Great Smokies. And, in the absence in those days of an interstate highway system, our trek always took us through Eatonton, home of Joel Chandler Harris, creator of Uncle Remus.

Fast food dispensaries were, like the interstate, a fixture of the future, and the thought (not to mention the expense) of eating in a restaurant was anathema to my parents, thus we used up most of the car trunk space to, in the words of my mother, "pack a picnic lunch." The picnic area at the Joel Chandler Harris Museum became our regular stopping point, and when I remember those summer road trips I always sense the cool concrete bench under my bare legs, the softness of Sunbeam bread collapsing in my mouth, the feel of thick green grass under my bare feet. And the laughter.

Oh, the laughter. Mama and Daddy with their best friends and traveling companions, Mr. John and Miss Frances. Me and Keith with their children. Everything was funny. Even the mishaps. It was summer and we were on a road trip and the trunk had been too full of sandwich meat and potato chips and powdered doughnuts to leave any room for seriousness.

Last Saturday I was back in Eatonton for the first time in probably thirty years. I'd been invited to speak to a women's conference. I arrived early, greeted my hosts, and got my bearings. I turned down an offer of coffee, explained that I take my caffeine cold and carbonated, and asked for directions to the nearest place open at that hour that could provide the same.

I'm certain that the directions were good, but the IGA to which I'd been pointed didn't come into view when I thought it should, so I kept driving. It had been a while, but I figured that Eatonton hadn't grown so much that I was going to get lost looking for a Diet Coke.

I was admiring the quaint shops in downtown, the well-kept yards in the Victorian houses on the side streets, when I came to a stop sign. Trying to decide which way to go, I realized that I driven right up to the Uncle Remus Museum. Thoughts of caffeine momentarily left me and I pulled into the parking lot. It all looked exactly the same—the picnic table, the log cabin, the statue of Brer Rabbit, and the placard of Brer

Rabbit with the big arrow tucked under his arm pointing the way to the museum.

I felt my face stretch into a smile. I felt my chest begin to vibrate with laughter. Under my long sleeves I could almost feel the summer breeze, could almost taste the Kool-Aid and the Pecan Twirls.

It has been a long time since I felt like a child. Actually felt in my body that lightness, that expansiveness, that wholeness that exists when you don't yet understand the concept of boundaries. When you have not yet experienced limitation or loss. When being certain is all you know.

And it has been a long time since I felt so scolded. Scolded because—it should be clear, I suppose—if the mere sight of this place where the innocence and security of childhood was epitomized can send me straight back to those moments, that posture, I should be able to get there at will. I should be able to remove myself, when need be, from the things and people that would steal my joy, kill my optimism, destroy my faith. All I have to do is remember.

It is almost Thanksgiving. The leaves that are left on the sycamore are limp and the color of cured tobacco. The ones that litter the ground at my feet are brittle and leather-brown, their edges curling like a hand making a fist. The marshals who enforce the laws of nature are finally, after weeks of effort, wresting those hands loose from their grip on summer.

I close my eyes and fold my arms across my chest against the chill wind, but under the jacket and the sweater, my arms are bare and I feel the warmth of June sunshine.

December 2, 2012

Once a month Lily takes heartworm medicine. It is a chewy, brown rectangle that, now that I think of it, bears a passing resemblance to the chewy brown rectangle of calcium that I take every morning. A long time ago Saint Buddy showed me a 3-D model of a canine heart infested with heartworms intending to make an impression. He did. So for twenty-three years—through Ginny's life and now through Lily's—I've dutifully administered what I've hoped would protect my dogs' hearts from becoming the living representations of that model.

I operate under no delusion, however, that either of them remained completely heartworm free. Ginny lived in the country, and now Lily lives there too. Running wild through fields, chasing down and scavenging wild animals on occasion, spending their lives outdoors means that one can reduce the odds, but not completely eliminate the chance of getting the one bite from the one mosquito that will infest a healthy beating heart.

And yet I try.

A few days ago I dropped by Saint Buddy's to pick up a refill. Whatever the number of cats and dogs present, I am always struck by the clean chlorine-y smell of the place—like a swimming pool or a freshly laundered white towel. It is the scent of competence, a perfume made from a mixture of science and compassion. It makes me feel safe.

Among the many angelic beings who spend their working days at Saint Buddy's is delicate and ethereal Amy, a near-doppelganger for a young Emmylou Harris. You can tell from the light in her eyes that she speaks the language of children and animals, and I am always glad when she is the one to take Lily's leash from my hand and lead her toward the treatment rooms.

As I explained to her the reason for my visit—to pick up heartworm medicine—she looked up from the computer and asked, "For Miss Lily?"

"Yes," I said and then laughed. "Though I could probably use some myself."

Amy laughed, too, and said something like, "Couldn't we all?"

Our eyes met. And held. And in that second, that two, three seconds, something important happened. A social exchange became a real conversation. A commonplace chat became a significant dialogue. An ordinary encounter became a memorable moment.

My laughter faded to a breathy chuckle. "Some days," I offered, "I'm convinced that my heart is absolutely full of worms."

Still smiling, but now less photographically, Amy nodded and said, "And if somebody offered me a pill for it, I wouldn't even have to have it wrapped up in cheese. I'd swallow it whole."

I've known Amy for a long time. We've spent lots of moments together. But this moment, this particular moment, I will never forget.

There was another woman at the counter. She must have overheard our strange back-and-forth, but she didn't acknowledge it. Just stood very straight, very still. I suspect that she was staring into a corner somewhere, pretending to be invisible.

I don't blame her. I've been her. I've been the woman without the time, the patience, the courage to engage in the bigger, deeper questions. I've been the woman who just wanted to get it done, whatever "it" was. Couldn't bear to think any more than absolutely necessary because I knew where thinking would take me.

But that never works for long. At least, not for me. I am convinced that we, all of us, are connected, and it is in having the conversations, sharing the moments, and telling the stories that we find the connections.

It is, in fact, quite possible that those connections are exactly the heartworm medicine humans need to live.

December 16, 2012

It is the season of wonder, after all. And, so, I have been wondering. Wondering how long it takes to decorate that huge tree at Rockefeller Center. Wondering how a person is supposed to learn all four verses of any particular Christmas carol now that school music programs are "holiday" performances. Wondering how our little part of the planet looks from the satellite that takes the photos for Google Earth when all the houses in all the cities and towns across America have their Christmas lights turned on.

But mostly I've been wondering who I am in this year's Christmas play.

One year I got to be an angel, but that was only because there were only two blond girls in our Sunday school class and the script called for three. I don't remember ever getting to be Mary, gazing beatifically at the baby doll that was wrapped in a flannel blanket and lying in a what somebody thought looked like a manger filled with a variety of hay that would never have existed in Bethlehem. (Directors, even when they are elementary school teachers, tend to typecast, and meek and mild has never been my strength.) Usually, I was the narrator, the one with the words.

Which makes it interesting that this year the character I'm feeling an awful lot like is Zechariah. Pious and proper, wise and mature, he's the one who couldn't bring himself to believe in a miracle and got struck speechless as a result.

Maybe it's just because I'm tired. Lots of time on the road, away from home, and the negotiation of more traffic and social conventions than I'd like is a slow but steady drain. Maybe it's because, in the last few weeks, a lot of people whose mortality I'd managed to ignore have become seriously ill or died. Nothing like a thinning of the generational cushion between oneself and ultimate vulnerability to give one pause. Or maybe, like Zechariah, it's because I've been paying too much attention to the acting and not enough to the experiencing.

Put on the priestly robes. Check. Walk respectfully into the sanctuary. Check. Light the incense. Check. Get out of there and go home.

Mail the Christmas letter. Check. Hang the wreath on the front door. Check. Get the gifts bought and wrapped and delivered and the parties attended and the hostesses thanked and...

Poor Zechariah. Doing exactly what he is supposed to do. Following all the rules. And he gets interrupted by an angel who offers him a miracle. But, because it doesn't fit into what he knows, what he expects, what everybody waiting in the temple courtyard knows and expects, he doubts, and because he doubts, his ability to tell the story is taken away.

Poor me. Doing exactly what I am supposed to do. Following all the rules. Have I been interrupted by the offer of a miracle and doubted? Is that why I'm feeling speechless in this holiest of seasons?

Like most miracle tales, Zechariah's ends not in silence but in cries of joy and shouts of laughter. The angel's promise materializes. An impossible thing is made real. And, finally, Zechariah gets to tell his story.

A story made better by the building tension of imposed silence. A story made more compelling by the passage of time. A story made timeless by the knitting of skeptical and miraculous, human and divine, earth and sky.

This year I am Zechariah. I am lighting the incense and listening for the whisper of an angel. And I will be silent until it is time.

December 26, 2012

It is eight o'clock on the morning after Christmas. One shelf of the refrigerator holds nothing but blue-lidded plastic tubs crammed with leftovers. The trashcan by the back door is stuffed with paper and ribbon, cardboard and plastic, tin cans and Styrofoam. The closet where I keep the wrapping paper is gorged with empty boxes that I will eventually find the time to break down and store until the next broad round of gift-giving.

Everything is full. Even the clouds. So full that they are saturated and dripping in heavy wind-swept drops over Sandhill. The road is slippery, but not very. Rutted, but not too. Muddy, but not markedly. The rain is hard, but the warnings of possible hail seem a bit dramatic. The weather is annoying and not much more.

It is now about 9:30. I look up from my computer at work and realize that the sun is out. The sky is a translucent baby blue, the clouds are high and white, and the puddles in the street look like mirrors. It occurs to me—not for the first time, of course—that it doesn't take long for the landscape to change completely.

The fraction of a second it takes to make a choice in anger that would never have been made in calm. To speak simple words that complicate everything—"It's cancer." "I'm going to have a baby." To pull a trigger.

I was driving home from Kate's graduation when I heard the news about the Newtown shootings. Just the night before, I'd been sitting high up in the stands at Kennesaw State watching her confidently stride across the stage to receive her master's degree. There was a little plus sign by her name in the program—honor graduate, 4.0 GPA. My heart swelled and my eyes watered and I couldn't stop smiling. It was one of those moments when the future was the largest thing in the universe.

In a few hours, though, that future—for twenty first-graders and six women who tried to protect them—would not exist. It doesn't take long for the landscape to change.

The light outside my window grows brighter and I think that, in a matter of days, a single stroke of the clock will turn one year to the next. Advertisements and fluff news pieces and conversations are littered with the phrases "new leaf" and "clean page" and "fresh start." We live as though change is voluntary, that it waits to be initiated by our desire, that we are never its victim, its passive object. In doing so, we live in deep denial of the fact that we are, far too often, powerless against the winds driving the clouds that empty the rain of adversity and pain and heartbreak onto our flimsy umbrellas.

Are those the only alternatives then? To convince myself that I can exercise and organize and meditate myself into perfect stasis, or give in to the reality that at any moment the foundations of my existence could crumble?

On Christmas Eve I watched intently as the presents were distributed. As each recipient accepted a package, Adam's son Jackson, two-and-a-half and an uncanny recreation of his father, hurried over to assist with the unwrapping. He reached up to touch the bright, curly ribbon first. "Ooooh!" he whispered.

His tiny fist grabbed at the taped seam on the box and pulled to hear the satisfying rip. "Ooooh!" he whispered again. And as the paper began to fall away and the contents came into view, there was always one final, elongated, "Oooooooh!" before moving on to assist with the next treasure.

That, I've decided, is the third alternative. I don't have to pretend I am in control or despair in the knowledge that I never will be. I can approach each moment, this present moment, as the gift it is. I can resolve to be amazed over and over again, acknowledging every change in the landscape with an appreciative, "Ooooh!"

Everything in this world has a hidden meaning. ...Men, animals, trees, stars, they are all hieroglyphics. When you see them you do not understand them. You think they are really men, animals, trees, stars. It is only years later that you understand.

Nikos Kazantzakis, *Zorba the Greek*

January 13, 2013

My friend died.

And I am hurting in a way that death has not hurt me before, a way that has nothing to do with my own mortality or lost opportunity or regret. Hurting in a new place, a place where the loss of adored grandparents did not reach, a place where neither the sudden, tragic death of a classmate nor the slow and brutal taking of a cousin dragged me. There is a gnawing in my gut, a gnawing to understand, to put to words the sudden numbness that seized me when I got the news and that faded at unexpected intervals over the next few days to leave me weeping.

On Sunday afternoon I found my way to the pew where we, the women who, as a group, go by any number of appellations but on that day were simply mourners, would sit together. We'd all worn red, Margaret's Wesleyan class color, in some form—scarves and jackets, dresses and jewelry—our mourning clothes splashed with the color of Valentines. We sat as closely as we could, shoulder to shoulder, trying and not succeeding to hide the fact that we were actually leaning on each other.

The congregational hymn was "Jesus Loves Me," and, having seen photographs of Margaret as a child, I could imagine her learning the words at Sunday school in Druid Hills. Learning them not just by memory but by heart, learning them in such a way as to carry that certainty with her right to the end of her eighty-four years. After the first verse, the words in the hymnal blurred into marbles rolling around the page and I left the singing to more stalwart souls.

The ministers who conducted the service knew Margaret well. We laughed when the senior pastor told the story of how Margaret had asked him why he did some particular thing and, after hearing his answer, replied, "Well, that's a dumb reason."

After reflection, he'd decided that, in fact, it was a dumb reason and adopted Margaret's suggestion for doing it another way.

We nodded when he explained that, upon joining the church, Margaret had insisted on being given something to do. "I didn't join this church just to sit here."

Near the end of the service, as the minister's words and the organ's notes and the bell's chimes mingled like some rare incense over our heads in the church's vaulted ceiling, I had a startling moment of clarity: With Margaret's death, there was one less person in the world who loved me. One less person who *loved* me. One less person who loved *me*. I suppressed the gasp that rose in my throat. I raised my fists to my eyes, now incapable of containing the tears.

Outside the church is a prayer chapel. Margaret took me there shortly after its dedication. I wrote about that visit, how after she had told me the architectural details, she had left me to be alone. Leaving her funeral, I walked up the narrow path to that chapel, noting the plaque at the doorway that indicated the date of dedication—five years ago to the day.

Inside it was exactly as I remembered. Candles flickered. Late winter afternoon light came through the high windows. The stone altar remained fixed, unmoved, unchanged.

I knelt, covered my face with my hands, and realized I had nothing to say. No prayer worth praying. No petition worth offering.

Then I heard it. The voice in my heart. Call her the Holy Spirit. Call her my true self. Call her Margaret. Call her whatever you want. This is what she said: "Love is all that matters. Love is all that matters. Love is all that matters."

And in that moment I understood. There will be no more endless amounts of food pulled from a seemingly bottomless freezer and no more endless rounds of Mexican Train Dominoes around a table in a mountain cabin. There will be no more picnics in Oakland Cemetery, no more nearly indecipherable notes, no more unsolicited advice. But Margaret's love is still here. Reminding, encouraging, provoking. Soothing, healing, holding.

And love is all that matters.

January 27, 2013

For the first time in days the landscape is still and silent. The wind chimes outside my bedroom, like icicles, hang hard and motionless. The fields, rolled out like bolts of unpressed linen, the edges fringed with caramel-colored broom sedge, are empty. No flocks of blackbirds to be flushed by the sound of a door being opened, a car being started. No dead leaves rattling. Just stillness. Just silence.

I pause. I wait. I linger for just a moment in the moment.

This place, this land, animates me.

Four days ago I stood on the beach. It was neither still nor silent. The water rolled onto the sand in low frothy waves, slapping at it like a kitten at a ball—teasing, playful. A brisk wind was swirling from the north end of the island, picking up the sand and tossing it in tiny eddies around my ankles. Its whistle, combined with the ocean's interminable shoosh-shoosh, accosted my uncovered ears, so that even my thoughts—thankfully my thoughts—were drowned out.

I paused. I waited. I lingered for just a moment in the moment.

This place, this ocean, it, too, animates me.

Can that be right? How can both the silence and the sound, the stillness and the stir, the earth and the water kindle that which lies within? There is contradiction and friction and tension between the two, but it is a necessary tension, the kind that allows an object on a string to swing in a perfect circle.

Mama's old Singer, the one on which she stitched all my Easter dresses and school clothes, every curtain that ever hung in our house, and enough dresses and skirts and blouses and coats for the women in town to fill a department store, had on its face a small protruding knob right over the needle. The tension knob, she called it, and explained that this knob regulated the length and tightness of the stitches that are made by the looping together of two threads, one from the spool and one from the bobbin. The spool feeds one thread from the top of the machine, spinning as the sewer presses the foot pedal. The bobbin, invisible beneath the throat plate, feeds the other.

She also taught me that you never ever touched that knob.

I didn't question the instruction, just followed it. But over time I learned that never ever didn't really mean never ever. Sometimes the tension knob needs to be adjusted. Making a buttonhole requires an adjustment in the tension. Using a decorative stitch or machine embroidery requires an adjustment in the tension. Pretty much anything other than simply attaching two pieces of fabric to each other necessitates a turn, sometimes an extremely subtle turn, of the tension knob. So what never ever really meant was "This is my machine and I adjust the tension, not you."

I think I am beginning to understand. I am stitching together experiences and thoughts and emotions to make my life. The spool thread is the land, the constantly visible strand that whirls and twirls so fast that I don't always notice it until it is suddenly still. The bobbin thread is the sea, less visible, but absolutely essential to the closure of each stitch. And the tension knob is my heart.

I haven't touched my sewing machine in years. It is in somewhere in the attic, back in the corner with my scrapbooks from college and a set of old deck chairs. I suspect that the belt has dry-rotted and it might take me a few minutes to locate a bobbin, but I am quite certain that muscle memory would direct my hand and wrist from the spool pin to the thread guide, down around the tension knob, up and over the thread take-up lever, down and back through the thread guide to the needle without a single deliberate thought.

Once you've learned to sew, you never forget. So it is with all important things.

February 10, 2013

The sign over my head identified it as the Express Lane. The crowd pressing around me suggested that the designation might be a bit optimistic. I wondered not for the first time what exactly had made me think I could not live one more day without banana bread yogurt and that, because I'd just left the gym, I was aptly armed to brave the Saturday afternoon mob of shoppers. There were, though, only two people in line ahead of me, so it was entirely possible that my good humor might actually survive the expedition.

The first of those two people was an older woman, probably seventy-five, her short white hair sculpted into layers of wide apostrophes at a weekly beauty shop appointment. Pale pink powder had collected in the wrinkles on her cheeks. She was paying with cash. There was probably a checkbook somewhere in her pocketbook, but there would never be a debit card.

Behind her was a young woman, probably twenty, her shiny black hair smoothed flat against her skull, her profile making me think immediately of those Egyptian coins with the images of Nefertiti. Her cheeks were smooth, the color of rich chocolate. She was purchasing one item, a box of Lemonheads.

The clerk handed the older woman her change, some bills, and quite a few coins. Her hand, deeply veined and wrinkled, shook with the involuntariness of age as she reached out to take it. With her other hand, equally contrary, she attempted to open her billfold. She struggled. "I'm sorry," she said to no one in particular and to anyone who might be inconvenienced by her difficulty. She was embarrassed and anxious and angry at her inability to make her hands obey.

"Here," I heard the Lemonheads girl say, "let me help you." She gently reached forward to catch the money that was about to spill on the floor, to hold open the billfold so that it could be dropped safely inside.

"Oh, thank you. Thank you." The woman sighed as she accepted help.

She put the billfold back into the pocketbook, grasped the handle of the buggy with both trembling hands, and turned to look at the girl again. "Thank you, sweetheart."

"You're welcome, ma'am."

Before I'd gone into the store, I'd been listening to a radio broadcast about the bombing of the 16th Street Baptist Church in Birmingham, the racially motivated attack that killed four little girls. I was not quite seven in September 1963. I don't remember the bombing, but I do remember, if only vaguely, a world of separate water fountains, separate entrances to the county health department, separate schools. And I remember the first black child to ride my school bus, how the older boys tried to bully him, how it made my nine-year-old blood boil, and how I invited him, a shy and quiet little first-grader, to sit up front with me.

Maybe it was the radio broadcast. Maybe it was the memories it conjured. Probably it was both that caused me to be so aware of what I'd witnessed in the Express Lane—the old white hands and the young black ones working together.

It has been nearly fifty years since Addie Mae Collins, Cynthia Wesley, Carole Robertson, and Denise McNair went to church one Sunday morning and never went home. It has been nearly fifty years since this country and each of her citizens were forced to reexamine the meanings of equality and justice. It has been nearly fifty years, and work remains to be done, but no one can deny that 200 million Americans don't remember "separate," not even vaguely, because they were not born under it.

The sermon that was to have been given at the 16th

Street Baptist Church on the morning of September 15, 1963, was titled "The Love That Forgives." I don't know if Rev. John Cross ever got a chance to deliver that sermon from a pulpit, but I have seen it preached over and over, most recently in the Express Lane.

February 24, 2013

As adventures go, it wasn't a particularly exciting, frightening, or life-changing one. In fact, most people wouldn't call it an adventure at all. I do because I define adventure as anything that requires me to do something risky or that interrupts my plans or even that I will at some point in the future have the opportunity to recount to some unsuspecting soul by uttering the words, "Oh, that reminds me of the day I..."

It happened like this: I'm leaving town for a couple of days, headed to Tallahassee to speak about and read from the book I wrote. I've gotten as far as Reidsville and stopped for gas. Tank full and iPod buds back in my ears, I turn the key. The Escape (aka the Bradley Fighting Vehicle) doesn't start. I try again. Nothing. Again. Still nothing.

I look around to make sure that no one is waiting for my pump. Deep breath. One more try. Failure.

That's okay. No need to panic. I have Triple-A. I walk around to take a look at the rear windshield where my Triple-A decal is barely visible underneath the road dust. I read off the 800 number and repeat it to myself as I walk back to get my phone. Triple-A answers on the first ring, and a young woman who was obviously hired because her voice is as soothing as a mother's hand on a fevered brow says, "First of all, are you in a safe location?"

Within two minutes a wrecker has been dispatched to a location whose address I did not know and which I could describe only by saying, "It's a Clyde's Market across the street from the courthouse." I notice that I am not nervous. My palms are not sweating. I am not imagining the horrible inconvenience it will be if I don't make it to the speaking engagement tomorrow. I am surprised at myself.

The wrecker is going to tow the Escape back to Sandhill and I need to locate other transportation, so I pull out the telephone book I keep in the sliding drawer beneath the passenger seat and open the Yellow Pages to Automobile Rental. I call four places. No one has a car.

I take a deep breath. And before I am consciously aware of what I am doing, I turn the key. It cranks! The Escape is running! Before it has time to change its mind I buckle my seatbelt, throw the phone book to the side, and pull out into the highway. I'm headed to Tallahassee. I won't stop along the way, and if the thing doesn't start in the morning I can call a cab!

I redial Triple-A. Another young lady with the same kind of voice answers. I explain that I no longer need a tow, that I appreciate their help, and that I hope she has a nice day. She returns the favor.

It is 196 miles to Tallahassee. That's a lot of driving time, a lot of time to think about what happened in the Clyde's parking lot. A lot of time to figure out exactly what made a situation ("car trouble") that is usually so aggravating, exasperating, and frustrating such a non-event. I consider the possibility that perhaps I have finally reached an optimum level of maturity, enlightenment, or detachment. I discard that possibility when I get behind an RV going forty-five miles per hour.

I discard a few other possibilities before I light on the theory that feels exactly right: I managed the situation rather than allowing it to manage me because of one thing—that first question the Triple-A operator asked: "Are you in a safe location?"

When the answer to that question is yes, whether the safe

location is a well-lit parking lot, a contented state of mind, or a trustworthy relationship, you are free to give your best efforts to solving the problem, formulating the new idea, creating something that has never existed before. You can actually think. There is no waste of energy looking over your shoulder or erecting barriers. There is no reason to hold things or people at arms' length and every reason to embrace them without hesitation. When the answer is yes, everything is an adventure.

March 10, 2013

I've been paying attention, the last few mornings, to the sunrise. I've broken the waking-up routine that normally follows my abrupt coming to the surface of reality by getting out of bed and, before doing anything else, opening the blinds on one window. For three mornings in a row I've stood there in my nightgown, bare arms breaking out in a rash of chill bumps, and squinted at the first beams of daylight like a newborn pup.

I couldn't tell you why. Honestly. I have no idea why it has suddenly become the thing to do, this bearing witness to the breaking of day.

What I can tell you is that the first couple of mornings I was just quietly awestruck, but the third morning, well, the third morning was different. Because the third morning the sky, instead of being streaked with its usual blood-orange and gold, was layered with hues of lavender. Closest to the horizon was a band of color close to that of spring's first irises. Above it was a swath of wisteria-hued mist, and above that was something akin to the shade of hydrangea that grew outside Aunt Tooster's house when I was a little girl. And above that, stretching up and out and over everything that is, was the palest silvery gray.

A few days earlier I had heard someone on the radio talking about a current off-Broadway play that examines the idea of living in the present, appreciating the immediate moment, something like a twenty-first-century riff on *Our Town*. The title of the play, as I heard it, was *Now Hear This!* and, in the nanosecond it took me to absorb and process the words, I thought it an appropriate title—a directive, a command, an order one dare not disobey.

The voice on the radio explained, however, that the title of the play is actually *Now. Here. This.*

Now. This moment. Here. This place. This. This work to which I have put my hands, this face to which I have directed my gaze, this love to which I have devoted my heart.

This one. Not another one. This one. Not the one that used to be or might be one day. This one.

Perhaps that contemplation was still lingering as I stood at the window watching the sky lighten. Perhaps that is why I did not, as I am wont to do in such moments, reach for the camera in what would be a futile attempt to capture the colors. Perhaps that, not the chill, is what moved me to wrap my arms around myself and hold tight. Now. Here. This.

Between blinks of my near-sighted eyes the colors began fading. The semicircle sun pushed its way into the day and I did, too. Dressed and drove across the newly deepened river to court. Manila folders and children in trouble and the language of the law became the now, the here, the this.

There is a temptation to linger in the lavender moments, to make them more than they are, to turn them into totems. One must be on guard, always, against the natural tendency toward tarrying until conscious living becomes unconscious languishing, against the propensity to seize the moment but never release it.

It is an unavoidable truth that now will become then, here will become there, this will become that.

The sun rose again today, its colors garnered from another part of the spectrum. They did not stretch out in layers, but spread in puddles over the trees, the fields, the grain bins. Another opportunity to stand at the window and stare. Another morning. This morning. This day. Now. Here. This.

March 24, 2013

On Sunday I went to the woods. To get there I had to walk along the edge of a just-plowed field, soft and uneven. At the back of the pond the field slopes sharply toward a creek that runs just beyond the property line, and my shoes began sinking into not-quite-mud. I ran to keep from being sucked in up to my ankles, gauging the size of the deer who had come before me by how far their hooves had sunk into the muck. The ground got solid again at the fencerow, barbed wire and rusted. I held it down with one foot and stepped across.

I went to the woods because it is close and quiet. I went to the woods because no one would know where I was. I went to the woods because I knew that my heart could breathe there. And my heart needed to catch its breath.

On Saturday I'd driven across the state to, as we say in the South, bury a friend, though he wasn't actually buried, but cremated. Brian was tall and strong. He had an Irishman's red hair and blue eyes that danced with the impishness of a leprechaun. He wooed and won my friend Melissa with bike rides and camping trips and songs played on a guitar, and, though I didn't meet him until the day of their wedding, I knew right away that it was good. Very good.

They had three beautiful children whom they allowed me and a lot of other people to love. They made a life that was wide and inclusive. And then Brian got sick. Sick with the kind of illness for which people don't set up Caring Bridge websites or organize blood drives. The kind of illness that you can't see, but that is no less real for its invisibility. And despite good professional help and lots of love—oh, so much love—Brian's life unraveled.

Sometimes people get better. Sometimes they don't.

Brian didn't.

On Sunday there were a lot of fallen trees in the woods. A lot of wind, a lot of rain over the winter had been hard on the old ones, the diseased ones. Most of them looked as though they had just sighed and laid themselves down. I walked down their lengths, holding my arms out to balance myself, bouncing just a little to feel the degree of rottenness in each.

There was one, though, that had splintered off about four feet from the ground. I walked over to peer inside the trunk. At first it looked just like the others—the layers of what I think Mrs. Foy called xylem all soft and dry, flaky like a Kit-Kat—but then I noticed that in the center there remained a small circle of heartwood. A modest ring of golden sap, glinting in the late afternoon sun that poked its way through the canopy. I leaned over to sniff the sweet tar scent. I stuck my finger into the cavity to feel the glassy hardness.

I couldn't help smiling. The pine tree had given in to the wind and the rain, but there remained, deep within it, a true heart.

At Brian's memorial service a friend of the family played the guitar and sang "The House at Pooh Corner," a song that Brian had played and sung for his two little girls over and over as a lullaby. In the quiet of the chapel, the sweet notes lifted up into the high ceiling and settled back over the heads of those gathered: "But I've wandered much further today than I should and I can't seem to find my way back to the wood."

Sometimes people find their way back. Sometimes they don't. But standing there—in my woods, on Sunday, remembering my friend—I realized this: wandering away, getting lost, forgetting the way home is never the end when the beginning was a true heart.

April 7, 2013

Beware those things, those people, that enchant you. As all readers of fairy tales know, enchantments are temporary.

I have been enchanted by moons—full moons, crescent moons, harvest moons, eclipsed moons—for years. I have religiously, as in with awe and in reverence, stood outside in cold that charged my toes like electrical current, in wind that deafened me to my own thoughts, in leftover heat that pasted my shirt to my chest, to look at moons the size of dimes and silver dollars, the color of ice and tangerines. I have laughed at, cried over, wondered at, marveled over the magic of gravity and seasons and tides.

Over the last few months, though, the moon has disappointed me. Almost without fail the full ones have been draped in heavy mist or completely obscured by clouds. The shiny crescent ones that have always before invited me to reach up, grab hold, and swing like a first-grader on a jungle gym have been dull and dangerously brittle, clearly not strong enough to hold the weight of my imagination. Even the one that was supposed to point me to the comet PANSTARRS last month failed. I stood in the side yard and stared and stared and stared without ever getting sight of what it seemed that everyone else was so easily observing.

So last week, on the night when the full moon was hovering over Sandhill, I deliberately stayed indoors. Took a stand. Made a statement. Protected myself against what I was certain would be another disappointing effort at channeling some of the magic of the sky into me.

I have tried this before. Not ignoring the moon, but protecting myself from disappointment. For years I proudly proclaimed that I was a vicarious learner, that I could watch other people and learn from their mistakes without the necessity of making them myself. I avoided risk at all cost, mistakenly thinking that the cost was insulation when, in fact, it was numbness. I took stands and made statements that did nothing but deprive me of the opportunity for joy.

I heard the other day that a better translation of the New Testament Scriptures generally called the Beatitudes would read—rather than "Blessed are..."—"You are in the right place when...." You are in the right place when you are meek and merciful, when you seek righteousness and make peace. When you are in a place of engagement. A place, I suspect, where it doesn't matter whether you can actually see the moon, but only that you are looking at where it is supposed to be.

The next morning I walked outside and was startled to see the moon, absolutely full, a huge white polka dot pasted over the western horizon. It was floating in a band of pale pink sky over a field of planted pines and a fencerow of scrub oaks. I stopped to stare. And in the stare was my apology.

She responded by remaining very still, hovering over her spinning earth, and covering me once again with enchantment.

April 21, 2013

Things wear out.

Over the past four months this very simple axiom has been demonstrated to me in the following ways: My office computer began the familiar slowdown that leads to the inevitable flashing blue screen and had to be replaced. The extendable handle on my office briefcase stopped extending and the briefcase had to be replaced. The glue on the crown on my front tooth that had stuck admirably for thirty years gave way and had to be replaced by an expensive implant. My washer and dryer, 27 ½ years old and never a minute's trouble, both stopped working within fifteen minutes of each other and had to be replaced.

And, then, of course, my dog died. On a fine spring morning when the morning mist had not yet lifted from the fields, Lily didn't come out of her house. Went to sleep and didn't wake up.

Nothing lasts forever.

But we want it to. We want something to last. The human heart is made of Velcro.

Earlier this week I went to a memorial service for someone I've known most of my life. At the visitation the day before, as I stood in a long and serpentine line to speak to his family, to offer condolences that I knew couldn't sound like much more than just another measure of a single song of sorrow, I watched as photographs memorializing this good man's life were projected onto a flat white screen. Whitewater rafting with his older brother and their sons. Gazing into the face of his newborn grandson. Sharing Christmas with his mother.

And then the photograph that brought me to tears. Five men, their arms around each other's shoulders, half-smiling at the camera held by one of their wives. Lifelong buddies. I know them, all of them. I knew them as boys. I watched them play baseball on Jaycee Field and football on Womack Field. I watched them grow into good men, good fathers, good husbands. I still watch them.

At the memorial service I sat near the back of the church. At the last amen, I watched the faces of the remaining four as they walked down that long, long aisle and back out into the world, a world without the smile, the laughter, the company of their friend.

I forget sometimes, when I go to the grocery store and don't see a soul I know, or walk a few blocks down the street and nobody blows his horn and waves at me, or meet someone for the first time and don't know a single person to whom she is related, that I still live among my people. I lose sight on occasion, when I'm watching too closely the construction of too many new apartment buildings, of the landmarks that are invisible to the natural eye but still show me the way. I get lost every now and then in the maze of newer, faster, better, only to get so tired that all I can do is sit down and wait for a familiar face to show up and remind me where I am.

There are a lot of reasons to leave the place that reared you. There are also a lot of reasons to stay. One of the best is that when we do, we get to remain a part of each other's stories, right to the end.

Nothing lasts forever. Except love. And friendship. And the memories of a shared lifetime.

May 12, 2013

I was walking in the woods, a hundred yards or so past the broken down, rusted out barbed wire fence that may or may not mark the property line between our land and our neighbors'. I had two friends with me, people accustomed to the outdoors, one of whom I call The Scientist. Their brand of nature, however, is generally more marine.

The one who grew up in Maine was amazed at the height of the pine trees and the size of the cones as we stood with hands on our hips leaning as far back as possible, chins stuck into the air trying to find the tops. The one who grew up farther down Highway 301 in the near-swamp was surprised to see so many prickly pear cacti peeking through the underbrush. They were both in awe at the elaborate armature of the deer stands that seemed to appear out of nowhere.

We were following old logging roads, still wide and open if well carpeted with years' and years' worth of pine straw. We had found the head of the creek that runs around the southwestern corner of the farm and identified a lone stand of wild indigo, its butter yellow petals folded like hands in prayer. And we were talking. Chattering really, as friends who haven't seen each other in a while will do.

Then, mid-someone's sentence, someone else called out, "Look! Deer!" We turned abruptly in the direction of the pointed finger. Not twenty-five yards away three deer were bounding through the woods, their pace unimpeded by the vines and logs and low-hanging branches that had made our progress slow and necessarily methodical. They looked like ballet dancers leaping across a stage.

And in seconds they were gone.

These woods are not unfamiliar to me. I have been here many times over the years, nearly always alone. The few times I've had company it's been just one other person and there have been few words between us. I have never before rustled up a deer.

My friends were delighted. I was rather pleased myself. It was as though the local fauna had decided to show off a little for the visitors.

Equivalent to my pleasure, though, was my curiosity. Was it just noise that startled the timid creatures and caused them to run? Were they really so afraid of something that was no threat? Or were they utilizing some sort of diversionary tactic to draw our attention away from where they had been? Was it possible that somewhere in the soft brown mattress of last winter's fallen leaves there was a newborn fawn or an old buck, sick and dying?

We tend to see people who run as deserving of contempt. We labeled them as men with no courage, women with no heart. We call them cowards and pray that we will never be so weak. The deer in the woods have made me wonder how many of those men and women run not for their own good, but for that of another. The deer in the woods have made me question whether running away might not, sometimes, be the best way of protecting something or someone that you love.

The last glimpse we got of the deer was a flash of tall white tail disappearing into the brush. We stood in the sudden silence for a brief moment and then turned for home, the questions rattling around in our pockets like pebbles and coins.

May 26, 2013

Adabelle Road was a little like Beacon Street this morning, only without Fenway Park and Boston Common. It was a pair of Canada geese, not mallard ducks, trying to cross the road with their offspring and, of course, there was no Michael the policeman stopping traffic. Still, the scene felt familiar as I was forced to a complete stop while an inter-gender discussion of which way to go took place on the white line running down the middle of the pavement.

After much flapping of the wings and shimmying of the hindquarters and moving onto opposite sides of the tight rope, the youngster, whose safety was the original focus of all the discussion before it disintegrated into what was clearly a domestic power struggle, fluffed up his own downy wings in a rapid flutter and startled his parents into making a decision and waddling out of harm's way.

One afternoon a couple of weeks ago I drove through the dirt crossroads, less than a mile from home, and saw a young deer standing in the middle of the road about a hundred yards away, tire tracks banding her delicate feet planted in the sandy earth. Something small, probably a squirrel based on size and speed, ran into the road and stopped directly in front of the deer. It seemed odd that a squirrel, or any other animal, unless rabid, would do such a thing. And deer are skittish. They do not pause in the middle of the road to investigate other animals. They are not curious about those with whom they share the neighborhood. It was odd.

I drove on toward the deer, expecting her to dart quickly into the forest. She didn't move. I got closer, within fifty yards. Still she didn't move. I was no more than twenty-five yards away when she finally trotted unusually slowly into the woods.

What I'd thought was a squirrel didn't move. I decided it must be a box turtle and that the movement I'd associated with it had just been a flash of sunlight through the canopy of pine trees. But when I got about half a car length away, I realized that the mound was a tiny fawn curled in on itself like a crescent moon. It was clearly newly born.

I stopped the car, opened the door, and started making shooing sounds. The little face stared up at me and the huge ears twitched the slightest bit, but he didn't move. "Please, little deer," I urged him, "get up! Get up!" He finally scrambled uncertainly to his legs. He was no more than two feet tall. After a wobbly start he ran ahead of me for about thirty yards, finally veering off to the edge of the road so I could get past and allow his mother, who'd done her best to divert my attention, to return.

It was a magical moment, and the images have flickered around the edges of my consciousness ever since I drove away. Encountering the bickering mallard ducks this morning brought the images back into focus and caused me to see what I had not before.

Making a crossing is fraught with danger. That which connects two parts of something is often where one is most vulnerable. A seam. An intersection. A joint. That is why there are reinforced stitches. That is why there are flashing lights and warning signs. That is why there are instruction manuals and trained technicians.

And, as in the cases of the fawn and the gosling, that is why there are those who have crossed before: because they know the way. More important, though, is that they know the risk. They know the risk and they go anyway, on guard not just for themselves but also for the ones entrusted to their care.

June 9, 2013

The morning after a rain, no matter how sparse, is always startling. It isn't just that every sprout and blade and leaf of green is greener. It isn't just that the vista has been swiped by a giant squeegee and everything is in clearer focus. And it's not even that the birdsong is deeper, as though the entire genus has overnight become a choir of contraltos. It's that some of the dust the rain has washed away wasn't clinging to the landscape. It was clinging to you.

I'd gone to bed with my head spinning. Not like Linda Blair's, but it might as well have been. And the spinning had no center. Like a lump of clay misplaced on a potter's wheel, snatches of conversation flew off in small clumps and landed on the floor. Unexpected memories sprang up and splattered my face. Futile attempts to separate lies from truth left my hands covered in slick mud. And my foot just kept pumping and pumping and pumping the pedal of the wheel.

As exhausted people do, I eventually fell asleep, though the spinning continued in my dreams. When the radio alarm went off at 6 a.m. with NPR alerting me to the fact that the NSA is collecting Verizon phone records of private citizens, it seemed obvious that neither my subconscious nor my unconscious nor any fairy sprinkling magic dust had intervened overnight to bring about anything like détente between the warring factions of my overloaded brain.

I showered, dressed in lawyer clothes, gathered up briefcase and purse, and headed out. Halfway down the back steps I stopped. Startled into stillness.

Every spring I am a little anxious as I wait to see if the hostas show back up, a little excited when they do. I watch their knife-blade buds slice up out of the ground, all tight and hard, and over the following days unfold into varied patterns of green and yellow and white banded leaves. I stop and look at them every morning to remind myself that resurrection is always a possibility.

What stunned me so this time was one hosta in particular, a smaller one. I could see that in its thick spade-shaped leaves it was still holding some of the night's raindrops, big and bulbous. They glittered in the morning light, looked like diamonds, polished and ready to be set into rings. In their

KATHY A. BRADLEY

smallness they reflected the light of the entire universe.

I could feel the spinning in my brain beginning to slow. I could feel the center beginning to take hold.

Last week the sweet and talented woman who wrangles my hair had a little extra time between appointments and suggested that we (meaning she wielding the flat iron and I doing my best to sit patiently for an extra forty minutes) straighten my mane. For the next few days I got a lot of attention for not looking like myself. No one said anything negative, but only Kate, like the child in "The Emperor's New Clothes," was brave enough to state the truth: "You don't look like Kap...not okay."

The most frequently asked question by those who recognized me was, "How long will it last?" And the answer was, "Until it gets wet."

That's what I thought of as I looked at the hosta, its leaves trembling slightly under the weight of their precious stones. How long does dullness hide brilliance? How long can selfishness masquerade as need? How long does deception prevail over truth?

The ground stays parched and barren until it gets wet. Clay is hard and useless until it gets wet. People can pretend to be something they aren't until they get wet. It is only after the rain has fallen, only after the tears have been shed, only after the tide has washed the shore that the sun has something in which to reflect its light.

June 23, 2013

A couple of Saturdays ago I was at Jackson's third birthday party. More unbelievable than the fact that he is already three years old is the fact that I am the great-aunt of a three-year-old. I had a lot of great-aunts growing up and my memories of them are consistent: they all had gray or white hair and they all wore plain cotton shirtwaist dresses during the

155

week and lace-collared shirtwaist dresses on Sundays and to funerals. Not one of them would have been found going down an inflatable water slide on my third birthday. Which is what I was doing shortly after Jackson blew out his candles and opened his presents.

Later in the afternoon, after a number of slippery descents punctuated by splashes and squeals and the realization that I really should have taken the time to put on some sunscreen, I noticed a slight burning sensation on my left elbow. I had, in all the flinging and flailing, managed to get the water slide equivalent of a rug burn, not a big one, just a small scrape. The next morning, though, I had the beginning of a scab. And by Monday, it was a genuine, irritatingly noticeable scab.

I am a careful person; some might say cautious. A few might even say overly cautious. The last time I had a scab was probably fourteen years ago when Ginny, unaccustomed to the leash I had to put on her to walk her into the vet's office, jerked hard and sent me tumbling over a wheel stop at the end of a parking space. For a couple of weeks my knee looked like I'd made a hard slide into home. I was particularly conscious of that scab, like the new, much smaller one on my elbow, because it was located on a joint and every time I moved it I was reminded of the pain.

About a week after the birthday party, when the edges of the scab had started to peel up a little and get caught on the bath sponge in the shower, I started thinking about the other kind of scab, the kind that forms on the wounds that nobody sees. Those hurts, the emotional ones, are so much worse and the amount of flesh torn off so much greater. The "wound healing reconstruction process" requires more than time and the replication of cells when what is damaged is a heart and the painful reminder comes with every beat.

Yet so often we are encouraged to treat the disappointment, the disillusionment, the loss of the dream as just another rug burn. "Give it time," we are told. "You'll get over it," we are assured. "It'll scab over," we hear and are meant to understand that the scab, hard and flaky, will miraculously numb the pain. Anyone who has ever felt the emptiness of disappointment or the loneliness of disillusionment, anyone who has ever watched a dream evaporate like a shallow puddle on a hot day knows that platitudes are worse than useless. They are infuriating.

They are also ignorant. Because platitudes ignore the last step: when the scab is gone, what is left is the scar.

Interesting thing about scars: they are made of the same protein as normal skin, but the composition is different. Instead of collagen fibers woven together in a random basket-weave formation, the fibers in scar tissue show an articulated alignment in a single direction. Scar tissue doesn't forget.

Some of those platitude people might see this as a negative thing. The reason it's not is that scar tissue, which doesn't forget, tells stories. The scar that runs up the back of my leg tells the story of the afternoon I led my brother and cousins on a tromp through the woods and fell on the barbed wire fence. The tiny scar on my knee tells the story of the four-year-old Kathy who daringly (and uncharacteristically) jumped off the front porch imitating some cartoon character. And, every single day, the scars on my heart tell me the story that I am braver and stronger for having survived the disappointments and disillusionments and dream deaths.

The scars are prima facie evidence that what I am is alive. And waiting for the next chance to go down the water slide.

July 7, 2013

The room was at the end of the hall. Its large windows looked out over an empty field where, during fire drills, we stood at bored attention in long lines awaiting the all clear. Its rows of desks were topped with heavy black Royal and Olivetti manual typewriters and worn copies of the Gregg Typing Manual that opened from the bottom rather than the side like ordinary books. The object, Mrs. Reba Clements explained to us on the first day of seventh grade, was not just speed, but speed along with accuracy.

At the end of the timed tests that eventually became as competitive as the sprints and free throws in P.E., we were required to proofread what we'd typed and count the errors, circle each one so that it stood out like one of the blemishes that had started to appear on our adolescent faces. Five or more errors and the words-per-minute count was simply irrelevant.

The English language, the placement of the letters of the alphabet on the QWERTY keyboard, and the unpredictability of the human mind inevitably and frequently create situations in which it is not only easy, but probable, that the rapidly twitching muscles in a typist's fingers will turn *was* into *saw* and *heart* into *heard*. Or *sacred* into *scared*.

Last year, within the twelve weeks that span my birthday and Christmas, three friends, all unbeknownst to each other, gave me the same gift: an hourglass. They are each about eight inches tall and contain sand that is the pale aqua color that I prefer over all others. I tried placing them together at first, but the concentrated reminder of life's ephemeral nature ("Like sands through the hourglass…") was too much for me, so, as with misbehaving children, I separated them. One is now in town at the office as a reminder that what I do there is not who I am. One is in the study at Sandhill, a functional prod to commit measurable time to the words that keep me alive. The third is on a chest in my bedroom next to a jar of seashells and a candle, a focal point where, at the end of the day or first thing in the morning, all the rays of thought and sensation and emotion can converge in a place of calm.

Last night, as I walked into the bedroom (Was it to empty my gym bag or put up linens or take out my contacts?), my peripheral vision registered something out of place. I stopped. Lamplight left the corners dull, but I could see that no photograph had been knocked over on its table, the door to the deck had not been blown open. All appeared to be in order.

I turned back to what I'd been doing and that's when I saw it: the hourglass, about a quarter of its sand still in the upper chamber and not falling. Time had, literally, stopped.

In the one to two milliseconds it took my brain to register the image and to relay back to my conscious self that clearly some object or force, most probably humidity, had acted upon the sand to impede its flow, my unconscious self, the one that is contained within but not defined by that brain and five feet nine inches of bone and muscle and flesh, the one that sees things that cannot be imaged and knows things that cannot be articulated, had already experienced the startle and fear of the possibility that time really had stopped and processed that fear into the marvel of expectation of the what-next.

What if there is only *now now*? What if I am no longer moving inevitably away from what I have known and inescapably toward what I cannot know? What if this—lamplight and the shimmer of new polish on my fingernails and the sounds of a baseball game on the television in the living room—is all there is? I am, for a moment, allowed a glimpse of what it could be like if I did not live caught between the magnetic poles of yesterday and tomorrow, feeling the equally violent pull of both.

I reach for the hourglass to dislodge the sand and am stopped. Leave it there, I am told. Leave it there and know what is possible.

I was always one of Mrs. Clement's students who aimed for speed. I pay more attention to accuracy now. It takes more than a couple of errant keystrokes to turn scared into sacred.

July 21, 2013

In the prideful insecurity and ignorance of my youth, I registered, in my first semester of college, for an upper-level history course. An honors upper-level history course. I was not alone in this risky venture but was accompanied by my friend since sixth grade, Lucy Lee. For the next four months, the two of us spent our Tuesday and Thursday mornings from 8:15 to 9:30 under the tutelage of Marcile Taylor, whose lectures we wrote down word for word, and took turns transcribing so that they might be memorized in hopes of passing the final exam.

Two totally unrelated facts learned that semester burrowed so far into my brain that thirty-nine years later they float to the surface on a regular basis at unexpected moments and, often, a propos of absolutely nothing. First: The single event that drove the settlement of the American West was the invention of barbed wire. And second: The single question around which the colonization of New England by religious refugees was conceived and carried out was the issue of how to live in the world without being of the world.

The invention of barbed wire tidbit has rarely been of practical use, not even in any of the trivia competitions in which I have distinguished myself over the years. On the other hand, the Puritan dilemma, as it came to be called, remains an unresolved quandary, an ever-present irritant, a never-to-be-lined-through item on the to-do list. And, to be honest, after all this time it nags at me not with regard to religious affiliation or practice, but rather as a question of how one manages to approach the world with an attitude of appreciation rather than consumption, how to experience intimacy with creation without experiencing the need to own it, how to inhabit a specific set of geographic coordinates at a specific moment in time in such a way as to know both without being changed by either.

Some days I am more barbed wire than thoughtful

Puritan. Some days I show up at the office locked and loaded with a tale about the ineptitude of the food service folks at my drive-through of choice or the cluelessness of other drivers in the line. Some days I bounce hard across the washed-out places on Settlement Road and wonder why I'm not a priority for the road crew. Some nights I stand on the deck staring at stars that look like the cheapest of rhinestones and want to throw what is left of my patience and my heart into the darkness that I am quite convinced is a bottomless pit.

But there are other days. Days on which I find myself mesmerized by the sight of a two-year-old in a seersucker bubble suit patting her fat hands together and bobbing her head so fast that her blond curls can hardly keep up. Days on which I notice that the dress I am wearing is the exact color of the cornfield reflecting the early morning sun, and I wonder if Sherwin-Williams has a shade called June Corn and declare out loud that, if it doesn't, it most certainly should. Nights on which I stand at the edge of the ocean, feel the waves carve away the sand beneath my feet, and hear my brain, my pulse, my heartbeat respond to their shush-shush-shushing like voices to a tuning fork.

Not long ago I got to watch Jackson as he got his first look at the ocean. Prepared to cajole and comfort, his mother and I stood on either side as I set his bare feet on the sand. He opened his mouth in a smile and ran toward the water, arms spread wide. The waves slapped at his ankles and he skittered away laughing. As they receded, he ran back out to meet them, to replay the slapping and skittering and laughing over and over again, all the while with his arms held out as far as they would go.

The Puritan dilemma was not resolved by the Puritans. It will not be resolved by the Methodists or the Presbyterians or the Druids or the atheists. Perhaps it is not even a dilemma. Perhaps it is the exact opposite. Perhaps it is a miracle—an amazing, astonishing, unexplainable condition that is still identifiably human, like bipedalism and the capacity for language, a condition that defies all known physical laws by demonstrating that everything that is can be held with arms that are open.

August 4, 2013

As a child regularly nourished by television Westerns, I did not realize that I was absorbing centuries-old literary motifs and archetypes. I did not yet have the vocabulary to recognize the heroic quest in the wanderings of various cowboys, but, like every human who ever sat around a fire inside a cave or a hearth inside a hut, I came to find comfort in the repetitive story lines and stock characters. That sooner or later one of the main characters would find himself or herself delivering a baby with no prior experience, or being the vehicle of redemption for some rotten scoundrel, exhibited not a lack of creativity on the part of the Westerns' writers but, rather, an understanding of the need to be reminded that no problem exists that has not been faced and solved before.

The other day I came across a contemporary poem, brief and pointed like a quick refusal, centered on the image of a snow rope. Reading the words—snow rope—sent my mind careening away from the poem to a montage of remembered images from all those Westerns I'd watched as a child. All of them, as I think of it now, whether set in Nebraska or Wyoming or Texas, eventually included an episode involving a horrible blizzard, an isolated homestead, and a snow rope, a rope whose one end was tied to a post on the cabin and whose other end was tied to the barn, a way to reach the animals without getting lost in the blizzard.

Inevitably, of course, the homesteader's hands get pulled away from the rope by the fierceness of the blizzard, or a child, wanting to be helpful, decides to go to the barn and can't reach the rope. Someone always gets lost in the blizzard.

At eight or ten, my only concern was what providential occurrence would save the hapless homesteader, the foolish child. Would Rowdy Yates and his horse stumble into the corral, drawn through the blizzard by the dim light in the window of the cabin, just in time to calm the hysterical wife and mother and charge back out into the maelstrom, one rugged hand on the rope, the other reaching down to pull the frost-bitten and nearly dead loved one from snow? Of course they would.

It had never occurred to me, before reading that poem, that we all have snow ropes. We all have practices, philosophies, people we trust to keep us alive as we venture out into the inevitable blizzards of life. The rope is sound, the knots are tight. We test them in the sunshine and we go on about our business.

And then it snows. Heavily. Unrelentingly. And, after a while, sitting inside around the fire becomes untenable, so we open the door and face the stinging cold and slapping wind, putting all our confidence in the snow rope. What we forget is that the snow rope is only as good as the grip on the hand that holds it.

I have survived blizzards, with my faith and my family and my friends braided into a cord not quickly broken, plaited into a snow rope stretched taut across an impenetrable landscape, but, in the end, I was the one who reached out, who grasped, who gripped with strength I didn't know I had and moved step by tenuous step through the blinding white. It was my choice to hold on.

Some stories end with the cavalry appearing on the horizon, with the cowboy showing up in the nick of time, with the marshal out-drawing the bad guy. But most of them end much less dramatically. Most of them end with the hero, or the heroine, realizing for the first time that that is exactly what he or she is.

August 18, 2013

The road did not always have a name. It was just a road, barely wide enough for two cars to pass in some places, dusty in dry times, slippery in wet. It connected two county-maintained highways, both of which had names but no road signs. People didn't often need directions out that way, but when they did they were given and received by landmark.

When we moved here in January 1974, becoming the only human residents on that three-mile stretch, Daddy went to see Mr. Fred Darley about buying insurance for the house. The insurance company wanted an address, a real address, something other than Route 1, Register. "We need a name for that road," Mr. Fred told Daddy. "How about Bradley Road?"

Daddy wasn't about to be that presumptuous and quickly demurred. He didn't need a road named after himself. "So let's call it Settlement Road then," Mr. Fred suggested, and Settlement Road it became.

Our first mailbox was up at the paved road, two miles from the house. Something about the postal service not extending its route for an initial period. Eventually it got moved to the crossroads, only a mile away. At some point the USPS decided we were there to stay and let us dig a hole and plant a box at the edge of the road right outside the front door. The mailman leaned out his window, stuffed the bills and magazines and sale papers inside the mailbox, and then turned around in our driveway to head back to civilization. It was a big day.

Our cars and trucks and tractors were pretty much the only traffic, except for the mailman, and the sound of an approaching vehicle always prompted Keith to the living room window to see who it was. Mama complained that her drapes got dirty from all the pulling back and peeking.

That was a really long time ago. The road is still dirt, dusty when dry and slippery when wet, but no one flinches at the sound of a pickup or a four-wheeler. We don't recognize every vehicle and, sadly enough, the drivers of some of them don't even wave when they pass. Just the other morning I had to wait at the end of my driveway for two cars to pass, noting with some surprise that neither of which was driven by someone related to me, before I could pull out into the road.

Along with my surprise came another feeling, one that lasted less than a moment but which I could describe only in ridiculously inappropriate terms: I felt trespassed, violated, even victimized. When had this road, this path for vehicular traffic, become so, well, public? When had my little piece of creation become so open to the rest of the world? How could I have missed it?

I did not pay a lot of attention to the surveyors who plotted out the tracts where other people now live. I did not really notice the distant sounds of the well-drilling equipment or the backhoes. I never looked all that far past the bend where the palmetto scrubs begin growing.

Change is never sudden. There is no single second in which the metamorphosis takes place, no twitching of Samantha Stephens's nose to blame. Not really. It is just the realization of change that is sudden. And sudden is painful.

To avoid that pain, one must pay attention. Be it weight gain or sunburn or the disintegration of a relationship, neglect and distraction and failure of concentration are at fault. To ward off the extra ten pounds, the burning red skin, the visceral ache of a broken heart, one must watch and listen, one must choose deliberately, one must do nothing by rote. That, if we want to eliminate the regret and sadness and panic that accompany every occurrence of sudden, is the challenge.

I am more careful now at the end of my driveway. I take my time in looking both ways up and down the road that did not always have a name.

September 1, 2013

One of them looked like the Jacob's ladder I used to make with a long loop of string laced in and out of the fingers of my two outstretched hands. One of them could have been a hammock tatted for a hummingbird. One, draped over the deck railing and onto the bannisters, was a net for flying fish, and all of them, all of the dozens of spiderwebs that dangled and hung and cascaded from every corner and edge of the landscape, were constellations, thousands of clear water stars the size of pinheads drawing archers and hunters, dogs and bears, crowns and serpents across the morning sky.

I am often caught up short as I walk outside first thing in the morning. While I have been encapsulated and cocooned inside my climate-controlled house, the world has been playing. Animals have danced in the darkness and left behind a wild confusion of footprints. Hard buds have softened and swollen and opened into flowers. The sun has silently bleached away the darkness and twisted it into a tie-dyed scarf whipped loose and left to float over the clouds.

But I had never been witness to such a display as this one. The entire backyard shimmered as the webs swayed almost imperceptibly. Dewdrops, strung like glass beads on filament, trembled in succession, the impish breeze turning them into dominoes. I pulled my camera put of my pocketbook and began snapping photographs, the rhombuses and trapezoids and wildly scalene triangles in the web designs made obvious by the zoom lens.

Each time I lowered the camera from my face I saw another, more elaborate web beckoning me to come, come see. And it is only because I heeded the beckoning that I walked up on the most exquisite, the most ethereal, the most splendid web of all. It stretched all the way across the double French doors that lead onto the deck. It attached to the overhead doorframe and the base of a chair sitting nearby. My arms, curved out and up and over my head, could not contain it. Unlike many of the others, it was round—not a compass-drawn circle, more like a hand-rolled pie crust—and its sections spread from the center like the spokes on a bicycle tire, delicate and shiny. Sheltered by the eaves of the house, it was covered in a lighter coat of dew, making its beading sparkle more like opals than diamonds.

After recording its beauty as best I could with the camera, I stood in the quiet dampness for a few more moments, breathed deeply, and wondered what might have become of the creature that had spun such a web. Then I went to work.

That night, I watched the full moon rise from the study window. The sky was less than clear, but I thought I could still get a good picture. I could sit outside and wait for the clouds to drift off.

The night noise was sucked into a cone of sound surrounding my ears as I opened the door. The warm moist air fell on my arms like a towel and I stepped out on the deck. Only one step and I remembered the spiderweb. The exquisite, ethereal, splendid spiderweb whose delicate strands were now caught in my hair and my eyelashes, stuck to my cheeks and my chest, hanging in sticky strings from my arms and legs.

For a moment I forgot the moon. I turned to face what was left of the transparent tapestry that had so enthralled me just a few hours earlier. The tender tension was gone; long loops of gossamer hung limp in the darkness. The symmetry was destroyed, the delicate balance gone. "I'm so sorry," I said over and over. "I'm just so sorry." I can't be sure whether I was apologizing to the long-gone spider or to myself.

I brushed the silky threads from my face and, in my repentance, felt the truth of the moment settle over my head: that which is beautiful, which took such effort and love to produce, is easy to forget if one becomes preoccupied with searching for the next beautiful thing. And perhaps it is in abandoning the exhausting search that beauty in all its forms finds its way to one's door.

Patience with each. Each in its own time. Time for all.

September 15, 2013

The anniversary has come and gone again. The anniversary of the day that became a hinge, when time bent into before and after. The anniversary of another day about which the sentence always starts, "I remember exactly where I was." And I do. We all do.

What I remember is being in Sky Valley with my mother, aunts, and cousins on a long-awaited girls' trip. What I remember is getting up and breathing cool mountain air, sitting on a second-floor porch with a view that rolled out in waves of all the different Crayola greens until it met the sky. What I remember is all of us laughing and talking over each other as we piled into the minivan to drive to Highlands and then stopped at the pro shop for JJ to buy Gregg a shirt. What I remember is JJ walking out with a bag in her hand and an inscrutable look on her face and words tumbling out so fast that it took all of us a couple of minutes to understand what she'd just seen on the television.

There are other hinges. The day in November 1963 when our second grade classroom work was interrupted by a sudden squawk from the brown intercom box at the corner of the blackboard and the crackly voice of an AM radio announcer said simply, "The President has been shot." The night in September 1972 when my exuberant monopolization of the family television for the purpose of not missing one single stroke of Mark Spitz's run at seven gold medals turned into a hollow-eyed vigil as Jim McKay, growing older by the moment in his yellow blazer, tolled the climbing number of deaths in the massacre of athletes at the Munich Olympics. The morning in January 1986 when I drove into the carpool line at First Methodist Preschool to pick up Adam, and his teacher could tell, because I was smiling and chattering away, that I'd not heard about the *Challenger*, how it had exploded into the bright blue Florida sky, how all those smiling, waving astronauts, including the teacher, were simply gone.

And other hinges. The non-historical ones. The ones that won't be found on a Wikipedia timeline. The ones that bent and crimped and creased time for no one but me. The days that started out like every other day and took detours I would never have expected or imagined.

We learn about time in units and, therefore, tend to see it as linear. One day follows another, one year comes after another. We say things like, "You never get a second chance to make a first impression" and "You can't unring the bell."

Hinges and our remembrances of them teach us that we aren't just marching forward in a straight line. We, as a species and as individuals, are actually spiraling, coming back again and again to the same people, places, and experiences, over and over because there is still knowledge to be gained. It is why, despite the universal desire for peace, there is still war. It is why, despite all we know about the things that cause illness and disease, there are still people bringing about their deaths by their own behavior. But it is also why Diana Nyad kept trying until, at age sixty-four and after failing four times, she swam from Cuba to Key West.

"We will never forget." The unofficial slogan of 9/11 remembrances. There is, though, a belligerence, a harshness, a quarrelsomeness to the statement that makes me recoil. I'd rather that we always remember. I'd rather that we lean into the bends in time, the creases in our days, absorbing them all so that, the next time around, we are full and strong and maybe, just maybe, ready to learn.

September 29, 2013

It is still September. Still September and I am startled on my Sunday afternoon walk by the tall skinny stalks of blazing star that have already appeared at the edges of the road. Florescent purple spikes, they sway in the breeze over the round faces of asters, yellow as grocery store lemons. It is not time for blazing star, and yet here it is.

I wonder if it's because of all the rain, the daily, drenching rain that made the summer feel so unfamiliar. I wonder if the tiny calendars inside the wildflowers have been thrown off by the fact that they didn't have to struggle for water, that their roots didn't have to stretch very far, that it was all so easy.

What I don't have to wonder, what I know, is that the blazing star, my favorite among the autumn wildflowers, will not last into late October this year. I will not be cutting armloads of the stuff at Halloween and filling my ceramic pitcher with the spiky stems to sit on the kitchen table next to a pumpkin.

We are a culture that reveres early. We extol the early bird who gets the worm and the early riser who is healthier, wealthier, and wiser than ordinary folks. We make ourselves feel more secure with early warning systems. We convince ourselves that with early detection we can outsmart disease. We have come to the belief, acknowledged or not, that we can supersede whatever other forces exist in the world—nature, divinity, time, other people—if only we get a big enough head start.

If we idolize early, we despise late. We almost always attach to it the modifier, "too," as though the very idea of late is excessive and distasteful. And, of course, we use it as a synonym for dead. So, when the language relegates that which occurs after the expected or usual time (the definition of late) to the category of undesirable, impermissible, or impossible, what happens to things that take their time, that meander, that do not hurry? How do we honor virtues like patience, persistence, and endurance if getting the worm is all that matters?

It is still September. But come October—October 1, to be exact—the Major League Baseball playoffs will start and Evan Gattis will be playing. So will 249 other players, but Gattis is different. He started the season as a non-roster invitee to the Atlanta Braves spring training, and his story has become well known since then: twenty-five years old and out of baseball for four years. In the eight years since high school graduation, while other young power hitters made their way through the college and/or the minor leagues, Gattis spent thirty days in drug rehabm three months in a halfway house, and two years working as a ski-lift operator, a janitor, and a golf-cart boy, among other things. After making his way back to college, he played one full season and was drafted by the Braves.

Most assuredly, people who knew Evan Gattis in the drug rehab or janitor days bemoaned the fact that he had lost his chance, squandered his talent, missed the worm. Those people were not in the stands at Turner Field on April 3, when Gattis homered off Roy Halladay, one of the best pitchers in the league, in his Major League debut.

The mother of one of my childhood friends once referred to her as a late bloomer. I'd not heard the phrase before and didn't understand at first what it meant, but there was something about it that resonated, something that I recognized in my eleven-year-old self.

I graduated from high school at seventeen, was practicing law by the time I was twenty-four, but it took until I was fifty-five to become an author, my version of making it to the big leagues. There were plenty of times when I wondered if I'd missed the worm, but the roots kept stretching through dry soil and hard earth and eventually a blade of green broke the surface and finally a leaf appeared and then one day there was a flower.

The blazing star bloomed early this year and has already begun to fade, but yet to come is the gerardia and the beautyberry and the ironweed. I can wait.

October 13, 2013

I crossed the room to say my goodbyes. The eulogies had been poignant and funny. The burial site, under a moss-covered live oak, was beautiful. The visit with the family was warm and uplifting. It was time for me to leave them in the tight knot of each other.

"Don't get up," I offered as I reached down to take his hand.

"No, no," he said, releasing me from a grip still strong. With one hand on the edge of the table and the other on the back of his chair, he began pushing himself up. "I want to tell you a story."

A story.

I had just been looking at a photo on the mantel, a black and white wedding portrait of him and his bride, handsome boy and beautiful girl. They were together for sixty-three years. Five children and fourteen grandchildren crowded the photo albums. There were lots of stories, but he wanted to tell me only one.

He turned from the table, curved his arm around my back, and moved the two of us away from the voices that rose, overlapped each other, and drifted out the doors toward the ocean. Propping his elbows on a high counter, he leaned forward and I leaned in, not wanting to miss a single word.

"Emily Dickinson wrote a poem about a hummingbird," he began. I nodded, more out of respect and encouragement than actual knowledge. "It goes: 'A route of evanescence / With a revolving wheel; / A resonance of emerald, / A rush of cochineal; / And every blossom on the bush / Adjusts its tumbled head, — / The mail from Tunis, probably, / An easy morning's ride.'"

The words rolled out with the ease of the oft recited. I could imagine him standing in front of his classroom of undergraduates, Philistines all, incapable of grasping the power in the spare words. He took a shallow breath.

"I put a hummingbird feeder outside Mary's window, and one day while the young woman who came in to help us...." He paused and raised his eyebrows questioningly. I nodded, this time with actual knowledge, to let him know I was aware of the role the young woman played. He offered parenthetically, "She was a lifesaver. We couldn't have done it without her," and then continued, "one day while she was there I looked out the window and saw a hummingbird at the feeder. I watched it for a moment and then said, 'The mail from Tunis, probably, an easy morning's ride.'" He was staring into the distance now. Watching his profile I could see the tears begin to rise in his eyes, hovering just behind the lashes, not falling.

He turned then and looked at me straight on. Wherever he had been just a second before, he had returned to the present. "The young woman, the one that helped us, she heard me and said, 'What'd you say?'" His cheeks rose up to meet his eyes and he chuckled.

I laughed. I could imagine the quizzical look on the face of the nurse's aide, the lack of comprehension, the wondering of what a hummingbird had to do with the mail. And I could also feel his sadness that, by then, the Mary who had understood his fondness for Emily Dickinson and who would have enjoyed the moment was lost, vanished somewhere inside the body that still required the care of this kind and tender young woman.

I have seen love before. Never before have I seen it more quietly yet eloquently expressed.

The leaves are turning and the days are getting shorter. It

will be months before the hummingbirds return, but I am certain that the first one I see will be bringing the mail from Tunis, a love letter from Mary to Hollis, sealed with a kiss.

October 27, 2013

The usually mindless twenty-five-minute commute to the office has required a little more attention the past few mornings. Crews of men in hard hats and florescent-trimmed vests have been supervising the cutting down of some rather large pine trees along the apron of U.S. Highway 301 South, and a little farther down another group has been digging troughs for, I assume, the long line of pale aqua pipe pieces that litter the ditch like massive tubes of penne. I suspect all of this is in preparation for the extension of utilities to property that borders the interstate.

It's probably about nine miles from the city limits of Statesboro to the interstate. Nine miles is a long way to send water or electricity or the digital signals that enable us to buy merchandise with the swipe of a plastic card. So now I'm thinking about how far we are willing to go for something we want, how far I'm willing to go for something I want. How far is too far.

It is suggested that we reach for the stars and that a man's—or a woman's—reach should exceed his—or her—grasp. The motto for the Olympic Games is "Citius, Altius, Fortius," Latin for "Faster, Higher, Stronger," a declaration that the athlete, and therefore mankind for whom the athlete is the idealized symbol, must be incessantly stretching and straining the limits of what is possible, never content with what is.

At the same time, though, we are admonished to live simply and modestly. A pair of ruby slippers in the Smithsonian, our national repository of culture, reminds us that the means to obtaining our hearts' desires lies not in some faraway land but within ourselves and that there is no place like home.

Can the dichotomy of the two positions be reconciled? Can both be true?

I confess to not remembering much from the two semesters of economics I took in college. Adam Smith. Opportunity cost. Guns and butter. What I do remember clearly, probably because it had immediate applicability to my life in answering the question of whether I should keep studying or get some sleep, is the concept of the point of diminishing return, the idea that at some specific moment, location, or cost the benefit of continuing in the same direction will be reduced. The problem back then—with the study or sleep conundrum—and now is always determining where, exactly, is that point.

I suspect that the men in the suits who hired the men in the hard hats have reams of data, stacks of printouts with colorful pie charts and lots of decimal points, confirming that their point is somewhere beyond nine miles, that the cost of installing all that giant pasta under the edge of a four-lane highway will be less than the eventual benefit of having jobs and a tax base that far from town.

I'm not so lucky. I don't have models and projections and pie charts available each time I'm trying to decide whether nine miles is the point at which I stop reaching and start grasping. There is no way to label the pros and cons of the various choices as constants, coefficients, and variables and then solve for x.

Most of the big decisions of my life are already made. Some of them turned out to be excellent choices, some not so good. What they all have in common is this: each one involved both reaching and grasping, not one or the other. Using my eyes to look as far ahead as I possibly could and using my heart to hold on to everything I knew to be good and true. Having vision and trusting experience. Not exactly a reconciliation of the dichotomy. Maybe something more like détente—an acceptance of difference and an easing of tensions followed by an acknowledgment of the equal possibility of both contentment and regret.

Perhaps that is the best one can hope for, along with the worst one should expect, which is the reality that, continuing to reach or pausing to grasp, one can never ever be absolutely sure.

November 10, 2013

Not long ago I was driving down a long flat stretch of highway listening to an interview of Billy Collins, former Poet Laureate of the United States, he of such soul-ripping lines as "You will always be the bread and the knife, not to mention the crystal goblet and—somehow—the wine." In the interview he kept saying things I wanted to remember, bits and pieces of sentences that I wanted to scratch out on tiny slips of paper and stuff into a phylactery and feel bouncing on my forehead as I walked through the day, phrases I wanted to tattoo on the undersides of my eyelids so that I might fall asleep staring into their mystery and contemplating their magic. Single words I wanted to turn into tropical fruit Life Savers and dissolve on my tongue in all their artificial color sweetness.

I've been trying to cut down on writing while I drive, though, so instead of reaching for the pen and pad I keep in the console, I opened this relatively new app on my phone. It's called Evernote. I heard about it from my preacher in a sermon he delivered back in the spring. (My church is cool like that. We talk about apps and stuff.) With Evernote I can speak what I want to remember into the telephone, and its amazing technology translates my voice into words and saves them in a computer file.

Billy Collins was saying that most writers talk about "writing what you know," but poets are different. "We write what we hear," he said. It was a succinctly beautiful line. I did not want to lose it. I picked up the phone, tapped the icon to begin recording, and spoke slowly and loudly enough to overcome the road noise. "We write what we hear."

I discovered later, when I got the opportunity to go back and review my dictation, that Evernote had some difficulty understanding my South Georgia drawl. "We write what we hear" had morphed into "we write what be here." I started laughing and then realized that, improper grammatical structure aside, there was equal truth in the scrambled version of the poet's declaration.

The breath of a buck blowing hard in the blackness at the edge of the deck. My own heart beating in rhythm to the pulse of one small star penetrating that same blackness. A voice, long silenced, reciting words long remembered. The breath, the heartbeat, the voice overlaid like tracks of music—brass over percussion over strings. Those sounds, those distinct vibrations moving through the air as waves that get caught by the curve of my ear and pushed through narrow fissures of tissue to a brain that then declares, "Remember that other night when...?" We write what we hear.

But at the same time, in the same words, writing acknowledges the existence of "what be here" and makes it real to both writer and reader. When words are stitched, strung, woven, or pasted together, the invisible becomes visible, the intangible concrete, the ephemeral lasting. It is why we excavate ruins for clay tablets and papyrus scrolls, present diplomas and proclamations, issue marriage licenses and birth certificates. We need to make a record to make our existence real.

Billy Collins wasn't speaking just for poets and Evernote wasn't mistranscribing just for me. With each thought and smile and sigh offered up into the world, we are writing what we hear. And writing what be here in this challenging, astonishing, mysterious world.

November 24, 2013

In the navy blue of just dark, the headlights illuminate only a few feet in front of the car. The high beams give shadows to the rocks on the road directly in front of the tires in outlandish proportion to their size, but the hundred-foot pines on the other side of the ditch remain invisible. Behind me the full moon is but a promise, not even a tease of her liquid silver light yet spilling over the horizon.

Just as I feel myself begin to lean into the bad curve, the arc of road where the beavers dam the creek every winter and the big aluminum culvert may or may not forestall the washing out of our little thoroughfare, a pair of yellow eyes appear at the lip where hard-packed dirt falls away to soft ditch. The eyes are too low to be deer, too high to be possum or armadillo. They have to be raccoon or fox, and it is too late, too dark for a fox to be out. Raccoon it must be.

I take my foot off the accelerator and feel the car slow as the lights pan the bend. The raccoon is standing on his haunches, tiny paws drawn up to his chest as though in supplication. He is young. I can tell by his leanness and the fact that his mask isn't very dark.

The number of raccoons, deer, possums, armadillos, foxes, and bobcats I have encountered on this dark stretch of road over the years is not one I can begin to compute, but I do know that every single one of them has behaved in exactly the same way: they have darted into the light. This one will, too.

So I wait.

He twitches. He jerks his head back and forth a couple of times. He makes a quarter-turn toward the ditch and, just as I am about to believe that this raccoon, this one creature out of all the creatures, will behave in a manner contrary to instinct and move back into the darkness, he bolts into the center of the road where the two yellow cones of light coming from the front of the car frame him like an escaping prisoner caught against razor wire.

Another infinitesimal hesitation and he is gone. Into the blackness that is the ditch on the other side of the road, into the night where just moments before he had been moving safely and leisurely.

The idea that light is safety is a generally accepted axiom of life. Most of what we fear is that which we cannot see. With light comes vision, with light comes a banishing of fear. And yet, at least sometimes, as with the raccoon, the urge to rush into light—to know everything, to be blind to nothing—does little more than invite danger and expose vulnerability.

This is what I am thinking as I accelerate once more and head toward home. It makes me shudder. I am a light-seeker. I navigate by looking for the sun to rise in the east and set in the west, by watching the stars. Feeling my way in the dark is not my way.

And now the raccoon is making me wonder: Is this the choice we must make? Do we choose to remain safe and in the dark, stumbling around over roots and rocks, chairs and coffee tables, ill-fitting jobs and passionless relationships? Or do we choose to become vulnerable and step into the light, exposed for all the world to see as small and fragile creatures, willing to challenge large and frightening beasts because life in the dark is not enough?

As I near home I notice that I can now make out the road yards and yards ahead, far beyond the reach of the headlights. The moon, round and ripe, is clearing the horizon. Through the brushy limbs of distant pines I see her clear face and feel her long slender fingers stroke my shoulder. Perhaps the choice is not what I had thought. Perhaps it is not light or dark. Perhaps it is not a choice at all but simply a learning that there is light within the darkness, a place where courage is respected, where fearlessness can be safe, where vulnerability is protected.

I go inside to bed and leave the blinds open. The moonlight puddles on the floor.

December 8, 2013

I was on the other side of the state visiting friends when my mobile phone produced the bell chime that sounds like an elevator reaching its destination. The message read: "Y'all might want to call in reinforcements, there's gonna be some property destroyed in the Boro tonight!" I knew what it had to mean, but the reality was so improbable as to deserve the descriptions it would get in the coming hours: unprecedented, unbelievable, miraculous.

26–20. Eagles over Gators. Georgia Southern over the University of Florida. David over Goliath. The No Smoking sign in heaven turned off just long enough for Erk to have a victory cigar.

Words began flowing out of The Swamp, words strung together into news stories and columns and blogs from the singular vocabulary and distinctive rhythm of sportswriters, words that would be trite and sentimental in any other context. And I read as many of them as I could find. After a while, because sportswriters are, first of all, good writers, it didn't really matter that I had not watched or listened to the game myself.

But I kept reading. The Facebook posts and the comments on the Facebook posts and the comments on the comments on the Facebook posts. It was all so much—I don't know—fun.

And then sometime around Tuesday afternoon, I think, I came across a blog post on the website "Gator Country," which identifies itself as "the insider authority on Gator sports." Written by Nick de la Torre, the post offered five things that stood out about the football game. Numbers one through four sounded familiar, simply recaps of all the other analyses I'd read. Number five, though, caught my attention. Number five was "Georgia Southern's joy after winning."

De la Torre described how, after the clock expired, the team in blue and white stormed the field. "A normal reaction," he wrote, "for a team that just pulled off an upset." He went on. "That wasn't the picture that stood out. The team circled around their band—yes, Georgia Southern brought their band (something even Vanderbilt didn't do)—and they sang their alma mater."

They brought the band. A team that most of the world expected to lose, a team that was out-manned and out-moneyed, a team that would be disappointed but not devastated to get on a bus and ride home having lost but done its best. That team brought its band. They brought the trumpets that heralded them as heroes and the drums that beat out the cadence of history. They brought music, that strange mixture of sounds that musters and rallies and holds together all manner of disparate souls. They brought the band because, while winning was what they came to do, it wasn't the only reason to be there.

That's where I stopped reading. That's when it stopped being just about football and started being about other things. About having dreams and pursuing them to the end. About making commitments and never walking away. About always bringing the band. No matter what.

In 1910, after leaving the White House, Theodore Roosevelt delivered a speech at the Sorbonne that contained what have arguably become his most famous words. "It is not the critic who counts; not the man who points out how the strong man stumbles, or where the doer of deeds could have done them better," he offered. "The credit belongs to the man who is actually in the arena, whose face is marred by dust and sweat and blood; who strives valiantly; who errs, who comes short again and again, because there is no effort without error and shortcoming; but who does actually strive to do the deeds;

who knows great enthusiasms, the great devotions; who spends himself in a worthy cause; who at the best knows in the end the triumph of high achievement, and who at the worst, if he fails, at least fails while daring greatly, so that his place shall never be with those cold and timid souls who neither know victory nor defeat."

If Theodore Roosevelt had been a football coach, I think he would have taken the band. To every game. No matter how far away. No matter how long the odds. 'Cause if you bring the band, there's always a reason to sing.

December 22, 2013

Right about now, "How ya doin'?" becomes "You ready for Christmas?" and my voice catches in my throat because, let's be honest, I never am.

The Christmas letter that has come to be expected could be written, reproduced, and mailed. (It has been.) The tree could be decorated within an inch of its artificial life. (It is.) The gifts could all be bought (Not quite.) and wrapped with tasteful paper and wired ribbon (I can only hope.). The refrigerator and pantry could be filled to brimming with multiple units of cream cheese and condensed milk and pecans cracked and shelled by the hands of loving parents (Praise the Lord.), and I still would not be ready.

Ready means preparedness and wholeness and availability. Ready implies fitness and qualification like an Army Ranger or a Navy Seal. Ready infers that I am somehow worthy to enter this holiest of seasons. No amount of wired ribbon or condensed milk, no number of empty stocking contributions, no measure of time spent reading Guidepost devotions can do that. I will ever stand at the edge of the stable wondering when one of the wise men is going to turn suddenly from his adoration of the baby and point me out as a fraud.

This is what I am thinking when some unsuspecting soul smiles at me in the Walmart checkout lane and asks, "You ready for Christmas?"

A few days ago, in the corner of a quiet coffee shop, at a table whose wooden top was scratched and watermarked, a friend and I bent our heads together in voices just above a whisper to talk about that, to confess what it feels like not to be ready for Christmas. "The season got here so quickly," she said. "Thanksgiving was hardly over before the first Sunday in Advent appeared." It has nothing to do with shopping or cooking or decorating, we agreed, but everything to do with stilling one's brain and filtering out the noise long enough to consider what it is we are supposed to be celebrating.

That is the difficulty. The stilling, the quieting, the letting go of the ill-considered notion that what I do, accomplish, carry out has some impact on the coming of Christmas, the coming of the Christ child into the world, the coming of the Christ into me.

I have been watching the moon these last few nights, watching it swell into a consummate curve like a pregnant belly nine months stretched. I have watched it, wondering with each rise over the edge of the darkening landscape, when it will be the perfect circle. It is a slow process, this coming of the full moon. It will not be hurried. It will not be slowed. It does not respond to my longing, my urging, my pressing.

I think of my friends whose first baby, a girl, is due to arrive any day now. They were told by the people who are supposed to know such things that she would be here before Christmas. Those people even suggested that they could make her come on a specific day, but consultation with baby Ella set them straight. She, too, will not be hurried. Nor will she be slowed. She is not withholding her arrival while her family gets ready. She knows that ready is what her family will become at the very moment they see her face, hear her cry, grasp her hand.

That is the answer. Ready is not something we make ourselves. Ready is something we become by virtue of that for which we long.

The moon will wax full, the baby will be born, Christmas will come.

In the long run the stories all overlap and mingle like searchlights in the dark. ...[M]y story and your story are all part of each other...if only because we have sung together and prayed together and seen each other's faces so that we are at least a footnote at the bottom of each other's stories. In other words all our stories are in the end one story, one vast story about being human, being together, being here. Does the story point beyond itself? Does it mean something? What is the truth of this interminable, sprawling story we all of us are? Or is it as absurd to ask about the truth of it as it is to ask about the truth of the wind howling through a crack under the door?

Frederick Buechner, *The Clown in the Belfry*

January 5, 2014

The wreath is still on the back door. The jingle bells tied to its branches reflect just enough of the floodlights at the corner of the house to make tiny blue and green starbursts. The ends of the big peacock-colored bow move only slightly in the night breeze. Christmas is over and I really should have taken it down.

My arms are full. I am struggling to find the key on the ring that holds too many. Once found, I am trying to fit it into the keyhole without dropping my purse, my briefcase, the box with the leftover lunch pizza. It slides in with some reluctance and I feel all my weight, physical and psychic, push against the door. Just get me inside.

I lean forward to let gravity pull the leather straps of purse and briefcase over my shoulder and down my arm to the floor. As I do, I feel something brush past my face, sweep lightly across my eyelashes. Too soft to have been the wreath or the wire-rimmed bow, too substantial to have been an errant curl. I reach for the light switch.

On the smooth white floor lies a tiny sphere of dark feathers. A baby bird. I gasp, knowing immediately that the tiny thing has been either hiding or sleeping inside the wreath and that I have rousted him from his haven. "Please!" I entreat the creature, crazily trying to loose myself of my coat and find someplace to deposit the pizza box before figuring out how I will get the visitor outside again. "Fly away!"

And he does. He obediently and politely flies away. Out into the winter darkness.

I catch my breath and think, That was too easy. It did not follow the pattern of my history with birds. And I do have a history with birds. Birds have made nests in my mailbox and my dryer vent; they have flown into and not been able to find their way out of my car and my house, the latter infesting the couch with a theretofore unknown insect, the bird mite, an unfortunate parting gift that cost me an exterminator's visit.

What I have learned about birds, lovely and melodious though they are, is that they can be troublesome. Challenging. Problematic. Gathering up the discarded burdens at my feet, I am relieved that this bird, this singular member of the avian community, has deigned to leave me alone this evening when all that is left of Christmas is cardboard to be hauled to the recycling station and leftovers to be dumped into the garbage and remnants of ribbon to be swept from the corners of the living room.

But he has not left me alone. He will not leave me alone. I keep feeling the light touch of the feathers across my cheek. I keep seeing his little body swell like a yeast roll rising in a warm kitchen, wings lifting him just high enough to get over the threshold.

And now I am thinking of the legend of the Christmas robin, the bird in the stable on the night the Christ child was born. I am thinking of how it is said that the wind blew hard and cold and the fire was about to go out when Mary began calling to the animals for help. The ox was asleep, the donkey was lazy, the sheep with all its wool was warm enough without a fire. Just as the fire was about to die, Mary heard the flapping of wings. A robin, it is said, heard the young mother's cries and flew to the stable to offer help. He flapped his wings at the dying embers until the fire was rekindled. To make sure the flames stayed alive, the bird used his beak to gather some twigs for the fire, which rose abruptly and burned his breast. The fire did not go out that night, and the breast of the robin remained red forever as a sign of his valor and selflessness.

I catch my breath again. This time I let it go slowly. My visitor has come in response to my call for help, the call that falls from every person who has ever woken up on December 26 tired or disappointed or just a little uncertain as to why she went to all the trouble or why he can't maintain the feeling of joyfulness all year long. The little bird has come to remind me that it is in giving that we receive, that it is in the presence of courage and sacrifice that love is born, and that the story will never end for want of a fire.

January 19, 2014

Once a year I find myself thrown into the crucible of one of the great debates of Protestantism. Getting the Christmas tree down out of the attic is easy, but getting it back up is something like one of the labors of Hercules. The steep stairs, the narrow opening, the weight and irregular shape of the tree itself, and the law of gravity create the laboratory in which I test the doctrine of eternal security. When at long last both the tree and I are lying sprawled in our particular states of disarray and exhaustion on the attic floor and I have not lost my religion, the annual experiment is concluded and I can proclaim, in a voice weakened but not vanquished, that God does exist and he is gracious.

This year, however, I decided that once the Christmas tree came down it was not going back up. My days of testing both myself and God, at least in that particular way, were over. The tree would, I asserted loudly and often, sit downstairs, its pieces in a pile, until I could obtain a storage shed. Sandhill is not a large house, and I knew it would not take long before the presence of a bristly green heap of faux evergreen became too irritating to endure.

Last week, after only four days of stepping over said bristly green heap in the dining room, I watched as a large truck delivered a ten-by-twelve-foot prefabricated barn to Sandhill. The gentleman driving the truck asked me where I'd like the barn deposited. Having carefully scouted the location beforehand and having ascertained the spot of optimum levelness within reasonable distance of the back door, I walked briskly across the yard and, like Captain Kidd showing the pirates where to dig, declared, "There!"

He'd been gone about fifteen minutes when I realized that I would have preferred to have the doors of the barn facing the road rather than the driveway, a ninety-degree difference in orientation.

I mentioned my change of mind to Daddy and, within a couple of days and not in the least to my surprise, he and Keith had a tractor hooked to the barn and were rotating it so that the double front doors with the big wooden X's on them and the two little windows on either side could be seen from the road. I wasn't there to observe the operation, but Daddy says that it really wasn't all that hard. It was just a small turn. And it made all the difference.

January is the month for resolutions, but, after seeing how significant that small turn was, it occurs to me that we might all be better served if we, like the little boy on AT&T's "It's Not Complicated" commercial who got his words confused, made New Year's revolutions instead. What if, instead of resolving, that is re-solving, solving over and over and over again, we choose revolving? You know, like the planets. What if we finally get over ourselves and figure out that orbiting is something we do around the center of the universe and that the center ain't us?

And what if we figure out that when we revolve, that is, when we turn, even slightly, it gives us an entirely different perspective? Turn the corner. Turn the page. Turn the tide. Turning turns things, inside out and upside down.

Turn around, and the shadow in which I've been walking becomes invisible. Turn loose, and my hands are free to catch hold of something new. Turn my attention away from the driveway that leads always to me, and I can see the road that leads to everywhere else. A small turn. It will make all the difference.

February 2, 2014

On Friday, leaving Darien, up and over the bridge that minds the shrimp boats, I ease my foot off the accelerator and let gravity pull me down toward sea level. The marsh spreads out on either side, at once embracing the river and wooing the ocean. What had been a rolling lawn not many weeks earlier, an endless swath of greenest green, has gone gold. Wispy grain heads waving in the winter wind, it is now a field unto harvest.

I note to myself that, despite heartstrings that need the tuning fork of ocean song to set their pitch, I am a country girl, and images of sowing and reaping come most easily to mind. I also remind myself that, it is said, the ability to use and recognize metaphor is what makes us uniquely human. I am glad to be human.

On Monday I notice that the fields around home are filling up with bales of hay, huge barrels pushed over on their sides. The whole world has gone gold. I notice and then I forget. On Thursday the telephone call comes. And the whole world goes the color of nothing. The light goes out, the prism breaks.

My friend has died. Died. I feel an explosion inside my chest. A real one. There is heat and pressure spreading from the place where my heart is cradled, where my friend has been cradled for nineteen years. Words are coming out of my mouth. I hear them, but I don't know who is saying them.

They, his family, want me to speak of him. They want me to stand up—on my own two feet, no doubt—and remember him. I say yes, even though I have no idea that I actually can. Later, when I am alone, I sit staring at the computer screen, the cursor flashing rhythmically, inviting me to begin. Where?

I glance around the room and my eyes fall on my faded and tattered copy of *The Little Prince*. Jim didn't know *The Little Prince* when I met him, but it didn't take long for me to share. And over the years most of our conversations included some reference to or quotation from that story. I put my thumbs to the page edges and the book falls open to the conversation between the fox and the little prince.

As I read the words I can almost quote, words I've been reading since I was sixteen and discovered that truth isn't necessarily factual, my breath begins to slow. My fingers begin to move over the keys. I can do this.

It is Sunday. I am standing up, on my own two feet. I open the book and I read:

> [I]f you tame me, then we shall need each other. To me, you will be unique in all the world. To you, I shall be unique in all the world. ...[I]f you tame me, it will be as if the sun came to shine on my life. I shall know the sound of a step that will be different from all the others. Other steps send me hurrying back underneath the ground. Yours will call me, like music, out of my burrow. And then look: you see the grain-fields down yonder? I do not eat bread. Wheat is of no use to me. The wheat fields have nothing to say to me. And that is sad. But you have hair that is the color of gold. Think how wonderful that will be when you have tamed me! The grain, which is also golden, will bring me back the thought of you. And I shall love to listen to the wind in the wheat.

It is Tuesday. It is Wednesday. The world is white. Snow, infrequent and puzzling, makes an appearance and we are gawking and fumbling and behaving in unseemly ways as though she were a movie star showing up unexpectedly at a family reunion or tailgate party. I am embarrassed a little until I am reminded that in the white are all the other colors. Somewhere in there is gold. The gold of wheat fields.

It will be a while—not Thursday or Friday or even next week—but the color will return. Gold will reappear. The winter sunrise, the spring daffodils, the summer corn, the autumn leaves will bring me back the thought of my friend.

And, having been tamed, I shall love to listen to the wind in the wheat.

February 16, 2014

The lines on the sailboats in the boatyard keen in the wind, cats meowing mournfully at some imagined wrong. The tide is low, the water nearly flat. In the not-too-distance a shrimp boat's silhouette cuts the gray landscape with edges as sharp as a knife blade. It is not exactly too cold for a long walk, but I am ill prepared; the coat is warm enough, the shoes sturdy enough, but without gloves or a scarf, my hands, my face, my ears will be gnawed raw in minutes.

I walk toward the water, the movement unconscious as a long-rehearsed stage direction. I stop at the just-edge, the rim where foam and salt lick the sand, where it is neither wet nor dry, where the waves sigh, give up, and move away in retreat.

I am here because there are things—events and words and feelings conjured by both—that, up to this moment, I have not taken the time to contemplate appropriately. I have held them like a bowstring, so long, so taut that my body trembles. Here, at the seam of my world, the place where earth and sea are stitched together, I hope to be able to let them go.

"What does it mean?" I begin, speaking aloud without any self-consciousness. "What does it mean?" I ask of God or anyone else who might, serendipitously or divinely, suddenly appear and have some thoughts on the matter. "What does it mean?" and I throw into the winter wind all the facts that I hold but can't seem to put together into a reasonable hypothesis.

I pause and take a deep breath. And another one. And another one. I hear the voice inside my head whisper, "There is a difference between the person who does not know how to love and the one who does but chooses not to."

I gasp. The whisper has released the bowstring, and the

vibration fills me.

At my feet there is an oyster shell. I pick it up, turn it over, am greeted by a tiny crab no larger than a nickel. Nearly translucent, with just a hint of veiny blue showing up near his tiny claws, he clings to the edge of the shell with his swimming feet, staring and daring me. I slide a fingernail beneath one of the little claws to see if he will grasp. It is what we do with newborn humans, offer them a finger and watch them circle it with their own.

I want this shell. I want to take it with me as a memorial, a reminder of the moment when the fingers of my weary heart loosed the bowstring and let it go, the moment when, standing here—at the place where nothing is unraveled, where everything is whole—everything I needed to know became clear.

But, of course, I can't take it. Someone has a prior claim. Not necessarily better, just prior. And in such matters respect must be paid to the one who got there first. "I will not take your shell," I tell the crab as I place it carefully back on the spot from which I drew it. I do not deem it necessary to point out that my greater power would have made it incredibly easy to do so.

My ears are beginning to burn. The movement of my cheeks feels disconnected from the rest of my face. It is time to go. I pick up half a sand dollar, its broken edge as even as the perforation on a postage stamp. It, too, is from this place. It, too, is from this moment. And no one else has a prior claim. This one can be mine.

March 2, 2014

The ice storm was upon us. The rain had been falling since the night before, and, in the cold cold air, the water had chosen not to drip from but cling to the branches and freeze. The power lines were drooping like the fluttering eyelids of a baby fighting sleep. It was time to get home.

But just in case there is no power when I get there, I think, I should probably grab a bite to eat. So it was that I was sitting at the window at Zaxby's, debit card in hard, when the lights went out. With no way to take my money and nothing else to do with my blackened blue salad with light vinaigrette dressing, the manager handed it over with a resigned smile. "I'll come back and pay," I promised.

"No need," he said. "Just fill out a comment card the next time you come in."

I carefully pulled out onto Fair Road, to which I refer as the Georgia Southern Autobahn, noticing immediately that the traffic light, like those at Zaxby's, was out. Cars coming from all four directions were inching slowly toward the center of the intersection, trying to figure out who had the right-of-way, when it was safe to accelerate. I quickly started counting in my mind the number of traffic lights between me and home. I caught my breath when I thought of the one at 301 South and Veterans Parkway. We were on the verge of chaos.

The verge of chaos. That narrow sliver of time during which one recognizes the impending loss of control and still resists it. That place within oneself where the way things are supposed to be is still visible, but fading. That physical sensation that masquerades as frustration but is nothing more than fear.

A friend of mine had surgery over the holidays. It forced her to cancel travel plans and miss seeing family. When she got back to work she couldn't find her rhythm. A few days after the ice storm she wrote to me, "I can't seem to catch up.... Is it me? Is it life? Everything feels so chaotic lately."

I wrote back, "Is it just awful of me to say that it's a comfort to hear you use the word 'chaotic'?"

I am uncomfortable with chaos. As a small child I was dismayed to see a can of Campbell's Chicken Noodle Soup shelved with the Chicken and Stars at the old Piggly Wiggly on South Main, and I wouldn't leave the aisle until I'd made sure all the varieties were in their proper orders. I am unsettled by everything from an unmade bed or a crooked picture to loud arguments between people I love. I am compelled to make the bed, to get out my level and straighten the picture, to mediate the disagreement.

The past couple of months, punctuated by unusual weather events and too many funeral home visitations and a round of antibiotics, have felt like nothing less than one interminable fit of chaos. Unmade beds and uneven pictures have floated at the periphery of my vision with nary a notice. So, awful or not, it was, in fact, a comfort to know that my friend was living through something at least a little similar.

My fingers paused over the keyboard for a moment. I took a deep breath, noticed the sunshine coming through the window. "But, then again," I typed, "I am reminded that in all the creation stories, chaos is what existed BEFORE...before the word is spoken, before the light separates from the darkness, before life arises. Perhaps there is hope in it."

I wasn't at all sure I believed it even as I hit "send."

That night when I got home I noticed the hydrangea between the deck and the carport. The hydrangea whose unpruned canes had condemned me every time I had walked outside since summer. The hydrangea whose shape had gone from full to skeletal. The hydrangea that, like everything else, had been coated with ice.

Sprouting from those ugly unpruned canes were buds. Chartreuse green, sharp-tipped buds. Living, hopeful buds. Pushing through the darkness, dispelling the chaos with the promise of beauty yet to come.

Southern Living says those buds will be blooms in late spring. I'm not certain when that is, but I think I can hold the chaos at bay at least until then.

March 16, 2014

I like punctuation marks. I like to know when something ends, when it's over.

Which is why this winter has just about driven me to the point of madness. It's been a sentence in a William Faulkner novel, winding capriciously from one place to another, picking up subject after subject with tentacle-like conjunctions and prepositions, offering jolts of unexpected discomfort with exclamations and interjections, creating confusion with unpronounceable words and unusual syntax.

It's been an Emily Dickinson poem. Lovely. At times. But more often difficult. To withstand. Or understand. Or even stand. On the ice.

In an ordinary winter I know that on New Year's Day I can clinch my jaws and hunch my shoulders against the coming cold and simply soldier through until the first daffodil appears along the ditch at the old house at the crossroads. This, however, was no ordinary winter. The dully cold days of January gave way to a foreign February, days of rain and ice followed by something impersonating spring that fled quickly in the wake of more rain and ice and wind.

And it wasn't just the weather. Three Friday afternoons in a row, I stood in a line at a funeral home visitation. On the Sunday after one of those Fridays, I stood to give the eulogy for one of my dearest friends.

When March arrived all sunny and balmy, it was clearly in disguise, but I was so eager, so desperate, really, for winter—outside and in—to disappear that I embraced it crazily, only to be betrayed once again as its true intentions were revealed as soon as enough windows had been opened, enough arms bared, enough shoes shed. Winter wasn't over.

I stood at the window looking at the first ruffly sprouts of leaves on the sawtooth oaks, laughing a little sarcastically at their audacity. Nature can be so naïve.

Then I noticed something I'd not seen when I got home the night before. The narrow strip of land between what passes for the yard at Sandhill and the branch that borders the pond, the little slip of woods where scrub oaks and bay trees, grapevines and Queen Anne's lace, kudzu and honeysuckle grow and meld into a particular ecosystem, had been burned off. The dead undergrowth that over the winter had created something like a choke collar on the trunks and stems was gone, and in its place was a flat black layer of soot and the faint smell of sulfur.

I suspect it was Keith who struck the match that started the burn—leaned over in the wind, cupped his hand around the tiny flame, and held it close to the tinder that would ignite all the debris. He stood there (I know this without having seen it) for a few minutes to make sure that the line of orange was moving steadily with the breeze, and then he left the fire to do its work.

It's what you do in spring. You ready the land for something new to grow by eliminating the last vestiges of the crop that was there before. It doesn't lessen the value of that previous crop, just brings it to an end. Adds a punctuation mark.

I stared for a moment at the black line. I thought I heard it say, "One cannot always depend on nature to signal the turn of seasons. Sometimes one must mark the change oneself. Sometimes one must decide and take action. Sometimes one must light a match, start a fire, and whisper to oneself, 'This is where it ends.'"

March 30, 2014

Jackson is almost four. That age at which he understands his separateness from other people but does not yet understand the separateness of his emotions. His will is clear and distinct, but his heart is still one with the world. Whatever is happening to him, be it highest joy or deepest sorrow, is happening to the world. That thing—the filter, the wall, the individuation of identity—that will eventually teach him that this is not so, that his feelings are uniquely his and not everyone can be trusted with them—has yet to take hold.

I am sitting on the curb watching him and his cousins jockey for position along the edge of the road as the St. Patrick's Day parade flows by. As soon as a float-rider's arm cocks back to toss a handful of Jolly Ranchers into the street, the three of them dash forward to scoop up the treasure. Other children converge from different angles, and the result of the looting and pillaging is not always an equitable division. As the youngest and smallest among the group camped on that section of sidewalk, Jackson does not usually return triumphant.

When he does, the plastic-wrapped corn syrup confection clutched in his little fist, he is ecstatic. When he does not, his hands empty, his shoulders drooping surprisingly low for a four-year-old, he is morose. The speed with which he moves from one expression to the other corresponds exactly to the speed at which the next float or tractor or pamphlet-distributing politician appears.

Driving home at the end of the day, my arms still holding the heat of the sunshine and my head the image of my sweet boy waving his arms to get the attention of the candy throwers, the parade turns into parable. I realize that, for Jackson, the candy was the object. Each time he was successful in gathering a piece or two, he quickly brought it to the curb and handed it over to either me or his mother. Once or twice he actually opened the package only to stick his tongue to whatever was inside and decide against it. But he kept going back, kept hurrying hard into the scrum of children. His prize, though he couldn't know it yet, was the participation.

People whose business it is to know these things—teachers and preachers, psychologists and seers—tell us that the need to belong is a fundamental human motivation, and it influences a wide range of behavioral and emotional responses. On Maslow's hierarchy of needs it is right there near the top. It is the impulse behind every dare ever accepted and the impetus for many a Las Vegas wedding and ill-advised tattoo. And Jackson has just reminded me that this craving, this insatiable hunger to be a part of something, doesn't suddenly appear in middle school. It is there from the very beginning.

It is also there to the very end.

My fingers are curved around the steering wheel and my eyes are fixed on the flat straight road before me. Miles ahead, the white lines on either side converge into a single point and the road disappears. The vanishing point. I am headed toward the vanishing point. For a moment I am acutely aware of Jackson's youth and my age, painfully alert to the fact that I may not be around to see his tattoos or hear the stories of the dares he takes or—please, God!—doesn't.

I take a breath. And with the breath the realization comes: this is what it means to be family. Belonging from the very beginning. Belonging to the very end. By blood or by happy accident. Without having to earn your way in. Without concern that you'll spend your way out. With the freedom to run into the street to grab whatever you can and the absolute assurance that there's a place to return even with empty hands.

April 13, 2014

I know exactly when I fell in love with sports.

The sky was gray; the air was chill. I was sitting on the living room floor, not yet tall enough to block Daddy's view of the sharp-edged console television on which the two of us watched a grainy black-and-white telecast of his and, thus, my Baltimore Colts. The players' legs, moving up and down in unnaturally sharp angles like pistons, were skinny. Their arms were even skinnier, protruding nakedly from the thick bottle cap of shoulder pads clamped down over each helmeted head.

I had engaged in this Sunday afternoon ritual long enough to know the basic rules, understand the most frequently called penalties, and anticipate the moments of high drama. I knew when commentary was appropriate and when it was better to remain dejectedly silent. The movements no longer appeared frantic or random.

But I was still learning, and Daddy was infinitely patient in answering whatever questions I posed. On this particular Sunday, the question arose as the quarterback (I don't remember if it was Johnny Unitas or the wannabe on the other team) dropped back to pass, and the entire defensive line charged toward him like mad bulls. The entire play collapsed and the broadcaster's voice, a scratchy baritone, floated over the room: "The blitz results in a loss of ten yards on the play."

Blitz. What a funny word. It sounded like a nickname for one of Santa's reindeer. It rhymed with glitz. And that malt liquor with the red bull on the can. It required lips and teeth and tongue in a rapid sequence that resulted in only one syllable. Blitz.

"Daddy, what's a blitz?"

"It's when all the players on the other team come after the quarterback. For that one play they don't have any other job."

I rolled it around in my mouth. It felt like something that would approach hard and fast. It tasted like something powerful. Blitz. I had just fallen in love.

Not long ago I came across another word I didn't know. I was reading a book about a spiritual journey and, though the author explained the word's definition and usage, I had to do my own research.

"Repechage" is used primarily in rowing. It is the method by which a competitor who loses in an early round is given another opportunity—a second chance—to compete later in the bracket. It's from the French word that means "fishing out" or "rescuing." It sounds a lot like grace. Port and starboard grace. Sculling grace. Sweeping grace. Grace in the middle of a cox and eight.

And what of baseball and its sacrifice? The runner's ultimate goal of making it home? There is grace, too, on a baseball diamond. And an ice rink. And a track.

I fell in love with sports in the moment of the blitz. The moment in which physical exertion for competition and entertainment became inextricably meshed with words (not to mention my daddy). Words that carry me far beyond the muscles and tendons that stretch and contract in extraordinary feats of physicality. Words that themselves stretch and contract in meaning and metaphor. Words that preserve and redeem and baptize all my days with grace.

April 27, 2014

It's a long, long way from toothpaste to peanut butter. One of them is in HBA, near the pharmacy and the front door where the buggies herd, and the other is in groceries, halfway between frozen pizzas and milk, nearly as far back as paper towels and eggs. I had the toothpaste in the canvas shopping bag that I had so righteously retrieved from the trunk of the car and was striding purposefully down the midway toward the peanut butter when I heard her.

"Hey!" She wasn't talking to me. "Hey!" Then again, maybe she was. I stopped and turned to see a little girl, between three and four, I'd guess. She was sitting in a buggy, legs dangling through the square steel holes. Her skin was the smooth brown of a Hershey bar and her eyes were round and dark.

"Are you talking to me?" I asked.

She nodded without smiling and then pointed to an empty buggy in the aisle ahead of her. "Why that there?" she asked.

The young woman I presumed to be her mother paused in her examination of the 50-percent-off Easter candy to figure out what the child was doing asking questions of a stranger. I gave the woman a quick glance, the glance that asks, "Is it all right for me to talk to your child?" I received in return the glance that says, "I can see you are not a kidnapper or child molester. Yes, you may talk to my child."

I took a step closer to the buggy. "I don't really know," I offered. "Now let me ask you a question. Why did you ask me?"

She shrugged her shoulders and tilted her head, lifted her tiny little hands so that she made me think for a moment of the Bird Girl in Bonaventure Cemetery.

"Do I just look like somebody who would know the answer to questions?" I teased. She nodded shyly. "Well, in fact, I do. I do know the answer to everything. Except that one question. I do not know why someone would leave that buggy in the middle of the aisle."

I took yet another step closer. "What's your name?" She looked quickly at her mother to get permission and then told me her name. "It's nice to meet you," I said, extending my hand. "I'm Kathy." We shook hands, waved goodbye, and I resumed my trek toward the peanut butter.

I wasn't all that surprised that the little girl would choose me, out of all the people passing her buggy on a busy afternoon, to approach. I was wearing a suit and high heels. I was walking purposefully. I looked like someone who knew what she was doing and where she was going. I looked like somebody with all the answers. When I am anything but.

What I am is somebody with lots of questions—not just ones like why do bad things happen to good people (though I confess that I struggle with that one as much as anybody) but also what possible difference can recycling my plastic bottles and soft drink cans make when I'm putting forty-eight pounds of carbon dioxide into the air just by driving to town and back.

And why is it so hard to give away books that I've already read and know I won't read again?

It occurs to me that I am not alone. Everyone I know walks through Walmart, through life with unanswered questions. That's not the distressing thing. The distressing thing is that we all dress and walk and act as though it were otherwise.

May 25, 2014

Sounding like Goethe on his deathbed, I handed the contractor the blueprints for what would become Sandhill and instructed, "Light. That's what I want. As much as possible." So the windows were broadened and lengthened in order to invite (not simply permit) as much light as possible into the rooms. With the serendipity of a southern orientation came sunrise through the bedroom windows and sunset through all the others.

I soon discovered that it wasn't only sunlight that welcomed itself into Sandhill through all those windows, but moonlight as well. Each month, in the week the moon waxed toward full, I would go to bed every night under a slightly more silver glow, and when the sphere of reflected light reached perfect roundness, the whole room shimmered. It was as though the pillows, the sheets, the comforter had all been sprinkled with sequins. As though a handful of stardust had slid down the moonbeams and scattered itself across the furniture.

Sometimes the light was liquid and poured through the panes like water from a jug or over a sluice or through a funnel, puddling on the floor and the bed linens in wading pools of pale illumination. I would lie there and listen to the silence, as full and content as the moon, and my next conscious thought would be morning.

For fifteen years there was not so much as a valance

adorning any of the windows. I loved the sun's play of bright and brighter overlapping each other on the floors, the strangely angled shadows projected onto the walls. I was constantly amazed that Old Linen, the paint color I'd chosen for every room, could look so completely different from morning to afternoon, from hallway to kitchen, from spring to fall.

The nakedness of my windows was both frightening and embarrassing to Grannie, who finally asked me one day, "Aren't you afraid somebody might be able to see in?" To which I responded, "If they come this far, they deserve to see something." She was not amused.

About eight years ago, in the aftermath of three bumper-car hurricanes that brought enough rain inland to require rather significant repairs, I put up blinds. Wide slatted ones. Easy to open so that I might maintain my this-is-freedom-not-vulnerability stance, but equally easy to close in order to seal off, block out, hide from view what I'd finally admitted in what passed for adulthood could be frightening, dangerous, or at least uncomfortable.

The result has been plenty of nights, many nights, most nights, when I couldn't have said whether the moon was waxing or waning or whether it was, in fact, outside my bedroom window at all.

Last week—and I can't say exactly why last week was different—when the moon was full, when the sky was cloudless, when the memory of moonlight shining through my window sprang up like a craving, I turned off the lamp and opened the blinds. I got into bed and lay still, waiting to feel the shimmer, waiting to hear the silence.

Across the room, on top of the chest of drawers, I could make out the silhouettes of photos, books, an hourglass. People, words, time. Their sharp edges were softened in the pale moon breath, dulled beyond any capacity to worry or wound. I had forgotten what moonlight can do to edges. I had forgotten what moonlight does to me.

June 8, 2014

About halfway between the communities of Adabelle and Excelsior is a creek bridge. On the Bulloch County side of the bridge, the county-maintained highway is known as Adabelle Road; on the Candler County side it is called Dutch Ford Road, though most of us who live nearby refer to it simply as the road to Excelsior. The two-lane highway, called by whatever nomenclature one chooses, has long been an obstacle course of potholes, washout, and loose gravel. The fact that the population of deer in the neighborhood vastly outnumbers the population of people adds to the overall perilous nature of travel on this short stretch of pavement. Its condition has been so bad for so long that there is, standing along the right-of-way, a tall metal flower, a diamond-shaped yellow highway sign pockmarked from flying gravel, that reads "Rough Road." As though it were not obvious.

Over the past few months in a rare act of county cooperation, or perhaps serendipitous synchronicity, both ends of the road have been resurfaced. It is now possible to traverse from US Highway 301, where Adabelle Road begins, well into Candler County on macadam smooth as ganache. A trip that used to strain the best shocks and struts, that could easily cause a blowout, that left drivers in need of chiropractic adjustment now feels like a ride down a waterslide. The finished product more than makes up for the brief delay experienced on the days when construction closed one lane or the other, leaving tractors and pickup trucks and minivans transporting farm laborers backed up around curves trimmed with narrow aprons and deep ditches.

The resurfacing has made the drive so pleasant that I can now pay attention to the environs. The deck that has been added to the back of the house in Excelsior. How many legs there are to the center pivot irrigation system in the field to the right. What is blooming in the yards of the farmhouses along the road.

This morning I noticed something else: the sign is still there. The rough road sign.

With all the scraping and regrading and filling of holes, all the tarring and rolling of the new surface, all the careful and tedious repainting of yellow lines down the middle, nobody thought to take down the sign. What was once a helpful warning to those who had not traveled that way before, what was once a gentle reminder to those who traveled that way often, what was once a important part of the landscape has become a relic.

Relics can be useful. They can teach us things about a time or place that we did not know. They can offer insight into the common characteristics between peoples of different times and places. They can remind us of progress made and progress still needed.

But a relic not recognized as such can be dangerous. We can spend so much time learning from the past that there is no time left to enjoy the present. We can hold on to reminders so tightly as to be unable to grasp anything else. And if an official DOT road sign tells you that the road ahead is rough, chances are that you will believe it and stiffen your entire body in preparation for being bounced and jostled and jerked. It is likely that you will clutch your steering wheel tightly and set your face like flint against nonexistent impediments.

I have no intention of violating Code Section 32-6-50 and taking down the sign between Adabelle and Excelsior, but I'm thinking of taking down a few others. The ones that keep me stuck in the traffic jam of destructive thoughts. The ones that force me onto detours that take me much too far from the path of my dreams. The ones that say "Do Not Enter" and "Wrong Way" and "No U-Turn." Especially the ones that proclaim "Rough Road" when all that lies ahead is possibility.

June 22, 2014

So bright that I could make out the fluted edges of geranium leaves. So bright that the rocking chairs glowed in the shadows of the porch. So bright that across the way I could tell, even in the dark of midnight, where the field ends and the woods begin. It was the first full honey moon to fall on Friday the thirteenth in almost a hundred years, an event that will not happen again, according to astronomers, until 2098, an appointment I will not be able to keep.

There was no breeze, not even the faintest tinkle from the wind chimes. Whatever songs being sung by the frogs and crickets and other night creatures were absorbed into the leftover warmth of the day. Bare feet planted on the top step, knees folded like a pocket knife to make a ledge for my elbows, palms splayed to make a ledge for my chin, I stared at the coin of the realm floating in the southern sky. I stared and breathed. Not deep, but full.

After a long winter, a season not just of cold and dark but also of loss—consecutive, repetitive, chronic—the last few weeks have been an invitation to rehabilitation. I have planted basil, pinched its leaves, and tasted spring in the pesto I made. I have created bouquets of sweet mint and peppermint picked from the plot at my back door, dropped their leaves into tall glasses of sweet tea, and sniffed with every sip the scent of green. I have cut bunches of hydrangea, filled Mason jars and Waterford crystal vases with their purple and lavender and pale blue puffs, and cared not at all that the tables got sprinkled with hydrangea dust.

I have done these things without thinking, without planning, without scheduling, and at some point the winter's bruises started fading.

Last weekend I got out the saw and the clippers. I started by trimming some low-hanging branches from the chinaberry and sycamore trees. That was just enough to work up a good sweat, so I looked around for anything else that needed cutting back. The rosemary at the corner of the deck, like so many things that we see all the time and, therefore, end up not seeing at all, had grown into a huge mass of dark green spikes and whorls. It had escaped the row of concrete edging and was well on its way to choking out the verbena, the pennyroyal, and the mint that shared its plot. A major pruning was in order.

I clipped and sawed and clipped and hacked. Stepped back to check the shape, snipped a little more. And all the while I was thinking about how much I like rosemary—its scent, its taste, its folklore. It has been known to repel witches and to divine the future. And it is, of course, for remembrance.

Which may be why, at some point when I paused to wipe my forehead, I remembered what my friend James had told me: Rosemary grows where strong women live. I stopped. "And sometimes it grows out of control, apparently," I wanted to tell James. Is it also possible that strength can grow out of control? That being the capable one, the dependable one, the reliable one can eventually, ultimately, finally become untenable? That strength can become not just a burden but a handicap? That it can do more than weigh down; that it can incapacitate?

In the winter, the winter of loss, I sprawled like the rosemary, moving in all directions to tend and mend and nurse and heal. I ran awkwardly over the boundaries that were meant to shape me. I did too much. I tried too hard. I was too strong.

I stared down at the rosemary and the raw, blunt edges of the branches I had so brutally cut. I bent down low and took a breath. It was the scent of evergreen. And that is for remembrance.

July 6, 2014

The snake was five feet long. Exactly five feet long. I know this because I measured the skin he left in the hosta bed right outside my back door. The skin he left in a soft pile like dirty clothes he expected his mother to pick up and toss in the laundry. The skin I picked up with a broom handle and stretched across the cool concrete carport, careful not to touch it because, well, you just never know.

I stood there and stared at it for a couple of minutes, thought about the snake wriggling and writhing and slipping out completely dressed in brand-new skin, wondered where exactly he'd gotten to after his costume change, and congratulated myself on having waited two days since the discovery before venturing close enough, with the broom handle, to examine what he had left behind. It was highly unlikely, I reasoned, that he would have hung around under the hydrangeas for two days, cool and damp though it would have been.

I was pretty sure it was a rat snake. Not because I am particularly adept at identifying reptiles, but because every time I've engaged Daddy to expedite the departure of a snake from the immediate environs of Sandhill, his swift and sure work has been accompanied by the remark, "Well, Doll, ain't nothing but a rat snake," and they have all looked like this one. But pretty sure was not good enough because this snake was still alive. Somewhere.

That is why I measured it. Went inside and pulled from the drawer by the telephone my Stanley 25-foot Locking SAE Tape Measure, chrome-plated and outfitted with a wide clip on the back to fit on a tool belt, an instrument one can trust when exactness is important. I stretched it out the length of the snakeskin, feeling the metal flex and flatten against the concrete, and locked it down where the skin splayed out in a ruffle where the snake's head had once been. Five feet. Exactly. I measured again just to make sure. Five feet.

My various Audubon guides are lined up on a chest by the front door, propped between sandhill crane bookends. I pulled out *Field Guide to the Southeastern States* and flipped to the reptiles section. On page 271, there it was: eastern rat snake, *elaphe obsoleta*. "Gray race of se GA west to MS valley is gray, with diamondback-like white-edged dark blotches." I peered through the thick plastic of the gallon Ziploc bag into which I had gingerly dropped the snakeskin upon bringing it into the house. The tiny overlapping scales, laid out like bathroom tiles, were the color of a summer thundercloud trimmed in unginned cotton. He certainly seemed to fit the description. But it wasn't enough.

Number. I wanted a number. And there it was: 5. The National Audubon Society had declared that rat snakes were 5 feet long. My snake was 5 feet long. Ergo, my snake was a rat snake. Held breath expelled.

There is some part of our humanness that makes us want to measure. To define with numbers. To identify in SAE terms. Not a bad thing when one is building a house or designing a rocket or even identifying a snake. It occurred to me, however, as I reshelved the Audubon guide and dropped the tape measure back into the drawer, that the ease of using numbers to distinguish one thing—or one person—from another can easily rob us of the other parts of our humanness.

Test scores that admit some students and leave out others without regard for abilities and characteristics other than test-taking aptitude, ticket sales that determine what is deemed to be art, descriptions like "age-appropriate" that cannot possibly be defined—they all ignore kindness and compassion and curiosity and courage and all the other numinous and luminous qualities that ultimately make houses and rockets, that produce schools and churches and families, that result in creatures a little lower than the angels, crowned in glory and honor.

I will leave my tape measure in the drawer by the door. I will keep the scale in the bathroom. I will maintain my checkbook register and watch my cholesterol and keep track of the time. But I will not be defined or limited or made afraid by numbers. Not even the ones attached to a snake.

July 20, 2014

I am lying on my back. The darkness outside the window has a green tinge, as though the night has mildewed. If there is a moon or any stars, they are blocked by the limp branches of the mimosa trees and the shed in the backyard, neither of which I can see, both of which I know are there. Also there is the clothesline where my mother hangs the wet sheets and towels that flap and flap and flap and come back inside dry.

I am in the top bunk, my face not far from the ceiling of the room I share with my little brother. He is asleep, curled into a comma in his cowboy pajamas on the lower bunk. Not far from his face are the red and green linoleum tiles that make the floor of the entire duplex a giant checkerboard. Sometimes I walk through the rooms stepping only on one color or the other. The tiles are big and it is not easy on four-year-old legs.

I am not usually awake in dark this dark. I am usually, like my brother, asleep, lost in Schopenhauer's "little death." But tonight is not usual. Tonight I am lost in what lies beyond the window, what lies beyond my street and the street behind it and the summer night heavy with humidity and the sounds of crickets and frogs and distant traffic. I am lost in something for which I do not yet have words.

It is the strange sensation of being in two places at once, of rubbing my arms and legs across the sun-dried sheets, of reaching out to touch the cool wall with my hand, of hearing the bunk bed creak when I roll over onto my side, while simultaneously drifting through the window and up and over the backyard, pulled by something strong and irresistible toward someplace. It is as though I am both myself and Wendy, for whom Peter Pan has flown all the way from Neverland to take back to the Lost Boys. How is that possible?

How could someone possibly sleep?

I cannot tell my father, who tiptoes in and peers into each of our faces in turn, who leans in close to hear our breathing, who touches our arms to assure himself that we are really there. I cannot tell my father that I am here and also somewhere else, that I have discovered, accidentally and haphazardly, imagination. I cannot tell him or anyone else—because I don't know it yet myself—that I will never be the same.

It is years later. A lifetime later. I am lying on my back. The darkness outside the window has a blue tinge, as though the night has frozen. There is a moon, but it is blocked for the moment by the languid flow of thick clouds. There is another shed in another backyard. The sheets against which I rub my arms and legs have never dried in sunlight.

I am often awake in dark this dark. Often gazing at a ceiling that hovers far enough above my face that I am reminded of my near-sightedness. Often carried away to a place that has grown as familiar to me as my hometown, though I don't always call it by its real name. I am more comfortable, in some circles, with saying that I am reflecting, daydreaming, or—God, forgive me!—brainstorming, but no euphemism, no circumlocution, no periphrasis changes the fact that what I am doing is imagining. And every last thing that I imagine is real.

I do not need a stocking-shaped shadow folded up inside a bureau drawer or a box of Turkish delight or a passport stamped Minas Tirith as evidence that I have been to Neverland and Narnia and Middle Earth. I do not need geological specimens from the thousand other places I created in order to establish their existence. And I have all the mementoes I want locked away in the warm summer night of my imagination.

August 3, 2014

I cannot say for certain what it was about the milk bottle that convinced me it was mine. It could have been the textured glass that felt like sandpaper. Or the way the sharp light from the windows at the storefront spread into a soft pool of translucence around its edges. Or the cool curves that conjured up memories of the mornings when my father left home early early early to make deliveries to the front porches of people I didn't know. Whatever it was, it took only moments for me to pay the exorbitant ransom and hurry away down King Street.

For the last fifteen years or so, the milk bottle has sat quietly on a shelf at Sandhill, the receptacle for quarters, a conservatory for the flat silver discs that clink their way into a mound of delayed gratification. When the bottle is full, I treat myself to something frivolous or, if not frivolous, at least a bit more extravagant than I would usually allow. Sitting on the floor, tilting the bottle just so, watching the quarters tumble through the mouth, feeling it grow lighter and lighter as it empties, I remember the little girl thrill of emptying a piggy bank. Stacking the quarters in towers of four, counting out the dollars, I am taken back to childhood Saturdays and McConnell's Dime Store and the Whitman Books display—a spinning rack where the Timber Trail Riders and Donna Parker and Trixie Belden waited for me and my insatiable appetite for words.

One morning while mindlessly brushing my teeth, I saw the bottle from the corner of my eye. And for the first time in ages I noticed the word etched in thick block letters up one side: WORTHWHILE.

It was, as I recalled, the name of the store from which I'd purchased the bottle, but in all this time I'd never really thought about it as anything other than that—the name of the store. In a single glimpse, though a sideways glance, I now saw with the clarity of a stare, a glare, a studied focus that it was more than a label.

Worthwhile, worth the while, worthy of the wait. It was a question. From its perch on the shelf next to the crystal clock and the ceramic angel, the bottle was asking me, "Is the container into which you are dropping your currency worthwhile? Are the things and people in which you are investing worth the while? Are the dreams you are dreaming worthy of the wait?"

I finished getting ready and headed out into the morning. The questions stayed with me like chaperones.

Sometime around lunch another question joined them when the voice of the poet Mary Oliver whispered in my ear, "Tell me, what is it you plan to do with your one wild and precious life?"

Wild? Not an adjective generally associated with me. Precious? I'll accept it but point out its substantial subjectivity. One? Ah, there's the rub. No argument available against it, no plausible dispute possible. One life. One milk bottle into which the coins of minutes and hours, days and weeks, months and years go dropping one by one. And as I tilt the bottle, as I watch the days and years tumble out at what feels like equal speed, on what will I spend them?

I spent the weekend on Signal Mountain with friends. On Saturday afternoon we found ourselves in a shop with a spinning rack that held greeting cards, not books. The five of us stood shoulder to shoulder reaching in and pulling out, reading to ourselves and each other the poignant, the clever, the downright funny sentiments.

I already had my hands full of selections to purchase when one of my friends said, "Here. This is you." She handed me a card quoting another poem by Mary Oliver: "Instructions for life: Pay attention. Be astonished. Tell about it."

Coincidences do not exist. I'd been asked a question and, failing to offer up a satisfactory or, really, any answer, the world provided it: What do I plan to do with my one wild and precious life? I plan to pay attention and be astonished. And with every moment that tumbles out of the bottle and into my hand, I plan to tell about it.

August 17, 2014

Why do we call it nesting? Why not denning or lairing? Why was the home of a bird, as opposed to that of a lion or fox or bear, turned into a verb?

Home from a weekend at the beach, I am scurrying to recover the equilibrium of my every day. The washing machine is swooshing with the first of many loads. What is left of snacks and drinks are scattered across the countertop, haphazardly emptied from tote bags and coolers, awaiting some decision as to whether they are worth keeping. I am standing on a ladder in the shed hoisting the beach chairs and umbrella up into the rafters. The last remaining grains of sand are a dry baptism on my head.

It rained while I was away, not much, but enough to leave the hydrangea surprisingly perky, the basil sprouting fresh green leaves, and the Russian sage, grown absolutely out of control at the corner of the perennial bed, drooping nearly to the ground. The rain was brought in by an eastern breeze; I can tell from the bits and scraps of botanical detritus littering the yard. Carefully watching my steps to avoid the holes dug by armadillos, I nearly trip over a nest.

Sitting perfectly upright, as though laid gently on the ground by soft hands, it is still balanced within the arms of a Y-shaped branch. I wish I had been there to see the branch, snapped brusquely from the chinaberry tree in the rain, fall? dive? float? down to the soft bed of grass on which it now rests.

It is hot. The shed has left me damp all over. My hair clings to my neck in wet curls and my shirt is stuck to my sunburned chest. I am honed in on the air-conditioned inside just a few yards away, craving the taste of just-made sweet tea in a glass sweating as much as I am. But I stop. I cannot resist the nest.

I bend down to peer into its perfect cup. Spun round and round each other like skeins of cotton candy, thin pine needles the warm brown color of melted caramel make a perfect inverted dome. Beyond its edge, larger pieces of brown grass, threads the color a tweed jacket I once had, form the exterior wall of the little house. Beyond that, twigs and sprigs thicker than spaghetti, not as thick as a pencil, lie across each other at odd angles like a game of pickup sticks.

There is no sign of its former occupants and, having lost its place in the tree, the nest is not fit for avian habitation any longer. I can, without guilt, requisition it for myself—a found treasure, a serendipitous gift. I stoop to gather it carefully into my open palms.

Why do we call it nesting, the instinctual need to adapt an ample and appropriate living space into a unique expression of self? What is it about the delicate configuration of stems and string and stray slips of paper, where eggs are laid and hatched, where raucous wars are fought to protect the hatched, where fledglings are set forth, that makes it a better metaphor for creating a home than the warren of the rabbit or the lodge of the beaver or the sett of the badger?

I carry the nest inside and place it on the kitchen counter where there is a basket of pears grown on Mama's tree and a hand-painted ceramic bowl I bought at the Club Mud sale at Georgia Southern. On an opposite wall is the framed blue ribbon Grannie won at the fair and a cross-stitched map of Georgia on which I added an extra X for Register. On every wall, on every tabletop, on every bookcase there is a bit or scrap of my life, and they have been spun and threaded together into a home. Into a nest. The place to which I return, the place from which I set forth again.

The lair, the lodge, the sett. The burrow, the den, the warren. Each is a digging out, an excavation, an emptying.

Only the nest is a building up, a construction, a filling. Only the nest takes bits and scraps, pieces and flecks, leftovers and remainders and turns them into a seamless whole. That is why we call it nesting.

August 31, 2014

What is this? A mimosa tree? Its slender branches are curved in an arc out over the ditch. Its fingerling leaves are dangling over my head. Its barkless trunk is all but hidden among the grapevines and pine trees and scrub oaks. I have walked by this very spot hundreds of times, driven by it thousands of times. How could I have never noticed a mimosa tree?

Memory overcomes curiosity and I can suddenly see the mimosa tree growing in the backyard of the duplex apartment where we lived when I was a little girl. Its branches dip so far down that even my four-year-old arms can reach those tiny little leaves. I love that they fold in on themselves when I touch them, coquettishly resisting my attention and, moments later, reopening invitingly as though to say, "No, really, I was only teasing."

In the shed there is a pink frying pan on the pink stove I got for Christmas. I break a branch off the mimosa tree, strip the leaves from the stem, wet them in a puddle by the back steps, and then dredge them in sand. I put them in the pink frying pan on the pink stove. I am playing house. I am having a fish fry. I would like to cut some of the flowers, put them in a Coca-Cola bottle as a centerpiece for my table, but I know better. The frothy filaments of mimosa blossoms wilt faster than morning glories.

But they are so beautiful, the color of deep pink associated with Florida and Silver Springs and swimsuits with halter tops and sweetheart necklines, things I have never actually seen, things I can know only from postcards and the labels on the big bags of oranges that the cousins from Florida bring with them when they come to visit. Once, Mama made a dance recital costume for a little girl that was just that color. It was made of satin, smooth and shiny like an evening gown, something else I had never seen. She sewed on every single sequin by hand, attached the ruffle of net onto the little derrière with stitches so tiny and tight no one could see them, and when it was finished she let me try it on and have my picture taken underneath the mimosa tree holding an umbrella made of stiff tissue paper and balsa wood.

Who knew the word "glamorous" at the age of four, but that's what I was. I knew it. I tilted my head and cocked my shoulder and smiled shyly at the Brownie camera, completely unaware that mine was not and never would be a dancer's body, oblivious to the fact that the satin stretched and puckered across my round belly, incapable of comprehending that the world was anything beyond that single moment. Itchy grass. Sunshine. Mimosa tree. Mama.

I realize I have stopped. I am standing in the middle of a dusty dirt road staring at a mimosa tree that is somehow the same mimosa tree that is growing in the backyard of my childhood. I am fifty-seven and I am four. I am wearing shorts and I am wearing a ballerina's costume that are exactly the same color. I am here and I am there. It is now and it is then.

Is it possible?

Madeleine L'Engle, she who taught me of time travel and tesseracts, once remarked, "Nothing important is completely explicable." This simultaneity, it is important. It is inexplicable. It is always and everywhere.

I will walk four miles before I return home. I will pass the mimosa tree on my way back. And in the evening breeze its leaves will quiver and send a wrinkle through time.

September 14, 2014

I found it in the back of a drawer. I had no idea how long it had been lying in wait.

The backs of drawers are dangerous places. There lie keys to locks I no longer wish to open and ticket stubs to movies I no longer remembering seeing or, worse, remember too well. In the far corners, worse than the mints without wrappers and the dead spiders, my fingers find souvenir matchbooks and fortunes from cookies folded like unbloomed roses. The backs of drawers are not mines; they are tombs.

And from such a tomb I pulled the disposable camera, Kodak orange, the kind I am not sure is even made anymore. The frame counter read 30. I couldn't remember: 30 taken or 30 left to take? Did it matter? It didn't.

Yes, the young man at Walgreen told me, the film could be developed. I would soon know what images hovered in photographic purgatory.

It is hard to remember the anticipation with which I used to drop off rolls of film, filling out the information on the thick paper envelopes: name, address, number of prints, glossy or matte. I knew where I had pointed the camera, knew what I'd hoped to capture, but had only a vague idea of what would appear on the 3 x 5-inch rectangles of slick photo paper. Sometimes I could wait until I got outside the store to delve into the package, most of the time not. The instant gratification of digital photography eliminates the disappointment of shuttered eyes and crooked grins, but it also extinguishes that little flame of excitement.

Which, in this particular case, was also tinged with anxiety. I've lived long enough now that it was possible that there could be images on that camera I'd rather not see, faces that could evoke sadness, scenes of places that no longer exist.

That my hands did not tremble when I opened the envelope is a truth. That I checked to see if they might is also a truth.

It took a moment, but only a moment, to recognize the skeleton of a building silhouetted against a summer blue sky. Sandhill, the brick already laid around the foundation, the framing done, the windows boxed, the trusses hoisted high like a teepee. Stacks of two-by-fours, a pallet of brick for the fireplace, and sawhorses scattered across the yard. A faceless carpenter straddling some beams.

Twenty-three summers ago the contractor dug up already-pegged peanuts to pour the footings of the foundation. Twenty-three summers ago Adam and Kate posed on the stacks of lumber and tried to get Fritz and Ginny, the golden retrievers, to walk the plank before the steps were installed. Twenty-three summers ago you still had grandparents living and you didn't have a cell phone and so many of the people you love now you didn't know existed. This is what the photos whisper.

One night, when the subfloor had just been laid but no walls were raised, when the whole house was one big open stage, I climbed up and walked through each room, arms raised under a silver summer moon, and blessed the house to come. Blessed all who would enter, all who would remain. Twenty-three summers ago.

The front door is a different color now, and there is a deck on the back. But the bay window still catches the sunset, the front porch the breeze. The deer still rustle through the branch when the back door opens and mockingbirds still fill the trees. Twenty-three summers have passed. Sandhill is different and yet the same. So am I.

The backs of drawers are prisons and prayer rooms, caskets and cathedrals, tombs and time machines. The backs of drawers are dangerous things.

September 28, 2014

A flock of blackbirds covers the field. Two hundred maybe. Silent and still before rising, as though at the lift of some unseen maestro's baton, into the air in one loud flap like a bleached sheet on a clothesline. I watch and listen and shiver. Blackbirds. Sign of cold weather.

Grannie said that. And every year, come fall and the first golden day in the 60s, come sycamore leaves bigger than my hand and the color of cured tobacco falling in layers in the back yard, come the rattling of peanut trailers and the drone of cotton pickers, I hear her voice. "Blackbirds. Sign o' cold weather."

Grannie was not a superstitious woman. Well, maybe she was: She didn't sweep out the back door after sundown and she didn't wash clothes on New Year's Day. And, for some reason we never figured out, we couldn't have fish and ice cream at the same meal. But superstition was a plaything. You could never really know. Unless you went ahead and washed clothes on New Year's Day and you got to the end of the year and nobody in the family had died. That was, however, an experiment she was not willing to undertake.

Signs, though. Signs were different. Signs were visible, audible, tangible connections to the world. One could plant and harvest and, thus, survive by signs. One could plan and hope and, thus, survive by signs. They were gifts of knowledge. Knowledge in a world where knowledge was scarce, where television had yet to be invented, where newspapers did not get delivered, where the only book in the tin-roofed house was a Bible.

And so she woke up each morning—babies at her feet and on her hip, cast-iron skillet in her hand—and looked for signs. A red sky meant bad weather was coming. Thunder in the morning meant "sailors take warning." And blackbirds meant cold was on its way.

I've been told that I look like Grannie. Once I caught a glimpse of myself in a mirror in a dark room—hair pulled back tight, no makeup—and a short shallow gasp left my throat. For a second I thought I'd seen her, long dead, walking beside me. Not long after, Daddy came in from the field and walked past a room where I was standing and stopped short. "My God!" he said, this man who uses the name of the divine only with reverence. "You look just like Mama."

But it is not just the large eyes and the straight nose, the dark hair. I look like Grannie for signs. I watch the sky, but I also watch people. I watch the birds, but I also watch the times. I listen to the wind, but I also listen to the silence, the words and the spaces between them.

What was knowledge for Grannie has become information for me, and information is not scarce in my world. I press a button on my telephone and ask Siri, "What is the temperature in Abu Dhabi today?" and in less than two seconds she tells me. (The high will be 100 degrees, the low 86.) Knowledge, though, that is still the pearl of great price.

What then are they signing, the birds who rise and circle and land again in one grand apostrophe? What is the message they telegraph in the black dots and dashes of their winged code? What knowledge lies within the whispers of their folding wings?

"All your life you were only waiting for this moment to arise."*

Watching. Listening. Shivering.

October 12, 2014

Eclipses are slow. Which means there is plenty of time to notice the dew on my feet and the armadillo hole I may or may not be standing in, to hear a strange choral performance by the frogs in the branch that sounds like a rustling of the feathers of

---

*"Blackbird," Lennon and McCartney.

a giant flock of geese, to get just a little impatient and start staring at the stars instead, making up my own constellations.

Eclipses are slow. Which means it is probably inevitable that I will end up wondering what it is about me and moons. Full ones, half ones, quarter ones. Waxing and waning ones. Harvest moons and blood moons and paper moons.

I remember the one that rose over the field behind Mama and Daddy's house as big and orange as a revival tent. I remember the one that spilled out over the ocean at Amelia Island, too tired to lift itself all the way out of the water. I remember the one that lit up my car with green light and followed me home from work and another one that hypnotized me through the windshield and caused me to miss my turn on the way home from Baxley. I remember them as though they are not all one moon, are not the same heavenly body spinning wildly and yet predictably through space around this heavenly body on which I am spinning wildly and yet predictably through space.

Moon myths are as old as man. My favorite may be the Inuit tale in which the moon, called Anningan, chased his sister Malina, the sun, across the sky every day, forgetting to eat in his pursuit so that he grew thinner and thinner. Not a completely logical explanation, but certainly a poetic one, and, in an age before telescopes are pointed toward the sky, the poet is revered above the scientist.

The thought crosses my mind like Anningan and Malina crossing the sky, arcing and falling. Filling and emptying out. Giving and taking.

Eclipses are slow. I decide that there is time to find my glasses, get the camera, record in some form the sky show. Coming out this time I decide that the porch is a fine enough place to stand, and I feel the wood flex and flex again under my bare feet as I shift to widen my stance, pull in my elbows, minimize the inevitable shake. I point the lens toward the darkening moon. The shutter clicks. I have captured an image, but I suspect that I have captured nothing to explain what it is about me and moons.

I also suspect that my friend the astronomer might tell me that pointing lenses—telescope or camera—is not supposed to explain humanity's love affair with the moon, but only to document it. I imagine that she might tell me that a knowledge of astrophysics would not assist me in articulating why I stay up late and get up early to stare at circles and half-circles and slivers of reflected light. I think, but cannot prove, that she would even be a bit perplexed at my need to try.

That may be why we still need myths, the stories that explain without logical explanation, the tales not of things that never happened but of things so important that they happened and still happen over and over again. And it may be why we need poets, the people who bid us to join them in the grass, throw back our heads, and stare at the sky.

October 26, 2014

The local, as in Savannah, public radio station is off the air right now as a result of damage from a lightning storm. Without the voices of Steve Inskeep and David Greene and—since it's October and the Supreme Court is in session—Nina Totenberg igniting the pilot light of my brain, I have been left to entertain myself as I perform my morning ablutions. So I sing.

I know a lot of songs. A lot. I can easily do a set of 1970s pop, American folk songs, or Broadway show tunes. I can do Streisand from all six decades. I can do traditional hymns and contemporary praise music (what my friend Phyllis calls "hippie songs"). This morning I found myself drying off, applying moisturizer, and brushing my teeth to the sweet and simple melodies I learned in Sunday school. "Jesus Loves Me." "Only a Boy Named David." And, of course, "Deep and Wide."

It's hard to sing "Deep and Wide" with a mascara wand in your hand. You have to fight the urge to do the accompanying hand motions, the vertical and horizontal extensions, and, once you get to the "fountain flowing" part, the swaying and finger wiggling. "Deep and Wide" is probably the first song I learned to sing, after "Happy Birthday," and I remember standing in front of the church and being particularly proud of the coordination I was exhibiting as we sang to our parents—remembering all the words and extending and swaying and wiggling at all the right times. All these years later there was something in me that felt the need to demonstrate my continued competency in that regard, but I was running late for work, so sing was all I could do.

Which is probably why I actually heard the words themselves. *Deep and wide.* Paid attention to the refrain. *Deep and wide.* Heard them and stopped to consider for a moment what they actually mean. *Deep and wide.* To my three-year-old brain the only possible association was literal. The deep end of the pool. The door left wide open. But to the woman standing before the mirror, the connotations were far less material.

Deep and wide hold associations positive and negative. Deep and wide carry the weight of a lifetime of dreams and experiences. Deep and wide are both rich and troublesome.

Human beings hunger for conversations and relationships that are deep; experience that is wide. And yet there remains something in us that demands ease and predictability, limits and boundaries. Like our brains partitioned into lobes assigned different physical functions, it seems that our psyches are partitioned as well. We may not be both Jekyll and Hyde, but surely where there is within us a place for City Mouse there is likewise a spot for Country Mouse as well.

Native American lore tells of the two wolves, good and evil, residing within the heart of man, and the answer to the question of which one prevails—"The one you feed"—may well reveal the only way in which deep and wide triumphs over shallow and narrow. Dive farther down. Sweep farther out. Drop the plow, broaden the blade. Feed deep, feed wide.

When I left home for college I had no intention of coming back. Deep and wide beckoned me with greater intensity at every mile marker. Deep and wide existed, in my mind, in places and people I'd not yet seen or met. My arms could not extend far enough to take them in.

For seven years I dug deep and I swung wide. I excavated my heart and stretched my mind deep enough and wide enough that, eventually, the territory I could claim encompassed that sandy piece of dirt and that great the cloud of witnesses that make up home. So I returned.

Sometimes, when a friend sets off on a great adventure or accomplishes some notable deed, I wonder what might have happened if my deep and wide had become far and away. Sometimes, when the burdens of the day press down on my shoulders like a fertilizer sack, I wonder what I might be doing if I had chosen shallow and narrow and followed a path someone else had forged. But sometimes, when the sun is setting and the tops of the pine trees look like paintbrushes set aflame and the deer at the edge of the field shine like burnished bronze and the rhythm of the rocking chair matches that of my beating heart, I don't wonder. I don't wonder at all.

November 9, 2014

There are so many ways to measure the movement of the year. The temperature of the breeze that comes wafting across the field, the color of the vegetation along the fencerows, the birdsongs or lack thereof. Each of them announces the passage of time from one season to another. But breezes and briars and birds can be deceptive. Wet summer winds can demand a sweater. Rain can make an autumn ditch run like spring. Birds can get confused.

Light never gets confused.

Sometime in the last week of August, I pulled up to the stop sign at the intersection of what Adam and Kate always called the middle-sized road and Highway 301, the thoroughfare Daddy remembers as a dirt road and I remember as a two-lane blacktop, which now fans out across four lanes and a median for most of its way into town. The whirligig of my mind was spinning from one thing to another: Would the 11 o'clock meeting end in time for me to make the 12 o'clock meeting? How high must the humidity be today to make those fat drops of water rolling off the roof of the house onto the hydrangea leaves sound like the flop of a big old toad frog? Should I stop for gas before work or after?

There was a lot of traffic. Both ways. So I had to sit still. I had to sit still and stare into the sun stuck just above the image of the horizon, and I realized it was not where it was the week before. It was casting longer shadows. Its color was transforming the sky from the clear blue-white light of summer to the mellower yellower light of fall. Already.

It was still hot at the time. Run the air conditioner hot. Walk barefoot to the mailbox hot. Wear sleeveless dresses hot. The geraniums on the front porch were still blooming. The leaves on the sycamore were still green. The peanuts were still in the field. It felt like summer still. But the light was saying differently. The light was not confused. The light knew that the year was waning.

I did not.

Well, actually I did, of course. I know how to read a calendar. But I chose to ignore the facts and live in denial of the inevitable, a situation that has left me this week rummaging through the closet in the guest room looking for warmer clothes, trying to remember how to work the heater in the car, and asking myself, as I scour the house for everything with an LED display, why exactly is it that I am changing all the clocks to a time one hour ago to re-experience again the hour I just lived. Believe me, there was nothing particularly worth reliving about that hour.

It is not the first time I have chosen obliviousness over enlightenment, ignorance over knowledge, unconsciousness over discernment. It is not the first time I have stood in direct sunlight and declared, "I don't see a thing." And it is not a big leap to predict that it will not be the last.

I wish it were not so. I wish that I, like light, could not be confused. I wish that discombobulation was beyond my capacity. I wish that no matter what happened I could count on myself to be "the natural agent that stimulates sight and makes things visible." I am not, though, a huge ball of flaming gases. I do not cast shadows and spark photosynthesis. I do not exert a gravitational pull on anything. I am a singular being who imagines herself motionless as she flies through space at over a thousand miles per hour.

I will never be light. I will always teeter on the edge of bewilderment. And, as I teeter, the best I can do is point my gaze toward the horizon and search out the sun.

November 23, 2014

I hit an owl.

The sky was dungaree blue, clinging to just enough light to maintain a horizon where the spikes of pine trees stood like arrows proclaiming, "This way to the exit." I wasn't driving all that fast. As soon as I saw him standing like a referee on the painted line in the middle of the road, I took my foot off the accelerator assuming that the sound of the approaching engine and the brightening headlights would motivate him into flight. It did.

He spread his wings and turned to face me. For half a second we were eye to eye. Long enough for me to recognize him as an owl, to see the wide-as-a-saucer circle of feathers around his eyes, to be transported by memory's subway pass to another time when my eyes met those of another creature and the world fell away. And then he flew directly into the grill.

I gasped, slowed, looked for a place to turn around, hopeful—How can a person be so hopeful?—that he had just been stunned and was even then fluttering drunkenly off to his nest to tell the story. "Honey, you ain't gonna believe..."

The headlights splayed out across the road in long white cones, and, along the other painted line, the one that divides pavement from ditch, I saw the feathered body, a still shadow. I burst into tears.

It was about time. The last week had been a painful one, a traumatic one. I'd buried two people I love, one a friend of nearly thirty years whose brilliant life had ended far too soon and one a woman whose long and fruitful ninety-one years had included her claiming of me as one of her own shortly after the death of my beloved Grannie. I had offered hugs and words of condolence, I had held hands and shared memories. At the latter gathering I'd even stood up in front of everybody, told a story or two, offered some scripture, and prayed. But I hadn't cried. Not really.

So now I did. And as I sobbed, gripping the steering wheel and blinking rapidly so that I could still see the road ahead, I turned on the owl, demanding loudly an explanation for why he had to fly straight into the car, a reason for why he should have been in the road in the first place, a justification for why he could not have delayed his kamikaze dive for the next inevitable pair of headlights.

Owls, it is said, are the only creatures that can live with ghosts. And they are, of course, purveyors of wisdom. I didn't really want to think that the women whose losses I was grieving were trying to speak. I mean, that would be a little too weird. Even for me. Yet there was something otherworldly about that moment when the owl locked his gaze with mine. It was as though I'd stumbled into a thin place, unknowingly wandered into land equidistant between heaven and earth.

The cell phone dinged. The peculiar ding of a text

message. I was almost home. There were no other cars on the road. I slowed to a crawl and looked down at the screen, one hand on the steering wheel, the other trying to get the tears out of my eyes so that I could actually read the words. But the message wasn't words. It was a photo of Jackson standing in the dim white lights of a just-raised Christmas tree, his four-year-old hand reaching out to place a candy cane on one of the branches, the profile of his expressionless face all curves and softness. He looked like an angel, all that blondness, all that cherubic innocence.

The tears resumed.

The denim sky was fading quickly, the pine trees disappearing into darkness. I leaned into the curve that hugs the pond where the Canada geese gather every morning and heard the voice of the owl whispering, translating for himself. "Life is tender, sweet girl. Life is tender. It is precious and must be protected, but it is fragile and must not be crushed. Hold it close, but hold it loose."

December 7, 2014

It is Advent. The season of wonder. Hot on the trail of Thanksgiving and Black Friday and just a few hours before Cyber Monday. And so far the only wonder I've experienced is what to do with two perfectly good pumpkins that, along with a couple of diminutive bales of hay, some cotton stalks and branches of eucalyptus, and about a dozen pine cones, made a lovely autumnal tableau for the front porch at Sandhill for the last two months.

It is Advent. And while I did manage to find the Advent wreath and the new candles I bought on sale at the end of last year, four tall candles with soft white wicks, I couldn't remember where the pink one goes so I had to Google it. And I decided that, in a world where people make Advent wreaths out of Legos, Mason jars, and/or pipe cleaners, I probably don't need to be too worried about whether the candle of joy is in the front or back, on the right or left.

The wonder I am experiencing is not awe and amazement or childlike anticipation. The wonder that has me by the throat is speculation and doubtful curiosity. I can't stop wondering why the focus in this season of preparation and anticipation continues to be on great deals and unbelievable bargains when, if we really believe the story, there's only the one, the one best deal ever offered. I can't stop wondering about the world's unanswered questions, failed intentions, disappointing behaviors long enough to feel the wonder of lighted trees and scented candles and welcoming wreaths.

But it is still Advent.

I am reminding myself of this when across the road flash one, two...six...no, eight, nine deer, long and lean, stretching out into the interruption of the headlights like dashes flowing from a fountain pen. There and gone. I sit at the mailbox for a few seconds longer, staring at where the deer have been, a circle of pale yellow halogen light hovering, quivering in an ocean of night.

In 1933, folklorist John Jacob Niles was attending a meeting of evangelicals who had been ordered out of town by the police of Murphy, North Carolina, when a girl, dirty and dressed in ragged clothes, stepped onto a little platform attached to a car and began singing a single line of a song. Seven times she sang for the price of twenty-five cents for each performance. In his autobiography Niles wrote, "[S]he was beautiful, and in her untutored way she could sing." From the single line that the girl sang over and over, that one fragment of melody, Niles composed the folk song that became the carol "I Wonder as I Wander."

A line in the second stanza goes, "High from God's heaven, a star's light did fall." Rolled out over the top of the car where I sit, still and alone, over the field where the deer fly silently in a herd, over the piece of dirt where all year long I wonder and wander, the stars' lights fall tonight. They are exceptionally bright. The sky is like a connect-the-dot picture. I get the feeling that if I can link one star to another to another to another something wonderful will appear. Something wonderful. Something wonder full.

I stare. Not hard. Not intently as though into a microscope, but with eyes wide and receptive. I can make it out now. It is the dirty ragged girl on the platform. The poor child with nothing to offer. I blink and then blink again when I recognize my own face. I am the one with dirty hands and feet, with patched clothes, with nothing but my untutored gifting and a craving to share with the world that which is inside. And I can do it only because I stand in the rain, in the reign of starlight pouring high from God's heaven on a too-warm December night.

It is Advent. I still don't know what to do with the pumpkins. Or any of the other things, tangible and intangible, that are left over from previous seasons, but I'm beginning to understand how to anticipate and prepare for the best season of all. I will keep wondering. I will keep wandering. And I will keep singing one line over and over and over again. Emanuel. God with us.

December 21, 2014

From the road, the wreath on the door and the swags over the windows look just right. From the road, they are even and balanced, the wire-edged ribbons are full and round, and the ends flutter just the least little bit in the winter breeze. From the road, the blue on the door and the blue in the ribbons match perfectly, and from the road the tiny white lights on the tree fill up the windows at the corner of the house.

But that is from the road. Up close you can tell that the swags are getting a little ratty and nothing matches perfectly and spiderwebs crowd the corners of the windows. Up close you can see that the porch needs painting and the shrubs need trimming. You can see big splats of mockingbird poop on the arms of the rocking chairs.

And when you go inside, despite the centerpiece of shiny glass ornaments on the kitchen table and the row of mercury glass votives on the sideboard and the pewter tray spilling over with Christmas greetings—stiff cardstock with your choice of matte or glossy finish—you will see that something is wrong. The tree, dressed in glass and shell and brass and stone, is dark along its bottom quarter. The lights on that widest and heaviest part of the tree have died, and no amount of jiggling of bulbs or pinching of bulbs or pulling out of bulbs has made any difference.

I am standing there staring, hands on my hips as though faced with a disobedient child, and wondering just how awful it would be to go through Christmas with a less-than-fully-lit tree. Not too awful really. I'm the only one who will be looking at it most of the time. And, like I said, from the road, well, it looks terrific.

That's when I realize that I can't do it, can't let the tree remain like this. I'm not a "from the road" person. Outward appearances aren't enough. Delicious icing can't make up for dry cake. A handsome face can't make up for a cold heart. Stirring rhetoric can't make up for failure to act.

At lunch the next day I go looking for lights. A couple of strands. One strand even. I walk into the seasonal department at Lowe's. There are huge swaths of empty concrete. I see two pre-lit boxed up Christmas trees, no more. There are no poinsettias. No towers of boxed ornaments blocking the aisles. There are no aisles. Just empty concrete. I feel the slightest bit of anxiety beginning to rise.

I walk a little farther and see a wall of lights. My shoulders relax only to tense up immediately as I realize that what is left are huge, twenty-first-century versions of the garishly bright glass bulbs that donned the trees of my childhood. I move slowly down the wall to discover that I would be in luck if what I wanted were icicle lights for the eaves of Sandhill or net lights for the shrubs. I would be a happy woman if I wanted solar-powered lights or crystal flickering lights. I am neither lucky nor happy.

Just as I am about to walk away I see a single box of 150 tiny white lights on a green cord. I reach out and grab them quickly, though there is no one else nearby. Only as I clutch them to my chest do I see the words "random twinkling" on the box. I don't care.

It is late when I get home, but I will not go to bed until the tree is done. I pull out the lights, dig around in the fake branches for an empty outlet, and start stringing. It takes only a moment to figure out what "random twinkling" means. About every fifth bulb blinks on and off at an irregular rate. Again, I don't care. I finish the stringing and step back, once again with hands on my hips, this time like a superhero surveying the universe she has just saved from extinction.

And then I laugh. I laugh at the random twinkling that is going on all over the bottom of the tree and in and out of the branches where I had to connect the cords. I laugh because I realize that, as it always happens, it has taken something completely unexpected and totally unholy to remind me what is going on here.

It's Christmas. And despite all our efforts to turn it into a visual fantasy, despite all our desires to maintain the impressions other people have of us as what they see from the road, it is always going to be a celebration undertaken by imperfect, broken, damaged people who occasionally get it right. Imperfect, broken, and damaged people who sometimes, every now and then, in the rare moment, exhibit random twinkling. And in the random twinkling make everything whole.

EPILOGUE

The morning after Thanksgiving I walked outside to look at the labyrinth stones, the ones in the flowerbed. The red lilies and purple irises that had bloomed with such primary brightness in the spring were long dormant, their bright green fronds reduced to limp brown strings of near-mulch. Months of grass clippings that had flung themselves from the lawnmower blades and into the beds were damp with decay.

The first stone I managed to find beneath the debris was the first one I'd found, the stone I'd been holding when I decided to build a labyrinth. I brushed away the grass and leaves pasted to its irregular surface by the mud of many rainstorms. I felt its hardness, its coldness beneath my bare fingertips, and pulled it loose from the grip of the ground. For a moment I was there again, before the choice had been made, in that wood on that path in that beam of golden sunlight.

"I want this rock," I had said. And so I had carried it with me back down a pebbly washed-out path, through a break at a locked and rusty gate, and out to a highway, realizing only then that we were leaving the wood by a different way from the one in which we had gone in.

I turned the stone over to look at the date. The careful strokes of the Sharpie, labeled clearly as *permanent* marker, were barely visible. The digits for month and day were gone. Only the year—09—was still clear. It didn't matter. I knew. I know.

One of the significant things about writing a newspaper column is that it keeps me conscious of the calendar, aware as I write that the words will appear in a medium known for its timeliness and that people expect seasonality.

Readers want me to acknowledge holidays.

What I have come to understand, however, is that all days

are holidays. They are all holy days. Not to everyone, but to someone. Each day of the year marks a moment of reverent remembrance—the day she was born, the day he died, the day she left, came home, broke his heart. The day the baby took his first step, lost her first tooth. The day the diagnosis came. The day hope was raised. The day hope was dashed. And because those days happen on a calendar, they happen over and over again.

And because time is a spiral—and not a circle—there is no closing off. There is no anniversary of happiness or sadness that brings an end to the original feeling. It is simply lived again each time on a different level, in the context of new experience.

I placed the stone back down into the flowerbed, the temporary home that had become its permanent resting place. The beam of light in which I stood five years later came from the same sun, but it fell on a different woman. I held my arms to my chest and moved toward the door.

What I have learned is this: Centered is not something I will ever *be*. The center is not something that can be contained within myself. It is, instead, a place. It is, instead a place, a place that I quite probably will never reach, but a place toward which I will always be drawn, by memory and desire, by reflection and duty, by grace and love.

The plan was to build a labyrinth. I thought it would be built of stones.

I didn't build it.

But I have built another one. It is the labyrinth of hours and days, the labyrinth of people whose faces I have memorized and whose voices echo with every beat of my heart. It is, in the end, a labyrinth of stories, each of which rises to speak with the force of legend and the authority of myth. I have collected them one by one, placed them along the spiraling path, and wondered my way to the center and back. Over and over and over again.

I have walked it on a long dirt road, down a sandy beach, over cobblestone streets. Down hospital hallways and courthouse corridors. I have followed its winding path again and again, one step after another, shepherding as best I can the unexpected events, the unruly questions, and uneasy thoughts that arrive along with the invited ones.

The deliberate and contemplative act of walking an actual labyrinth, the physical movements that I had imagined would mesh body and spirit and leave me enlightened, the slow and purposeful wandering toward a literal center and back out again has become, instead, a slow and purposeful *wondering*. Gathering scraps of thought and crumbs of ideas, adding flecks of recollection and shards of unexpected insight, I have performed the alchemy that turns wondering into words.

That is the labyrinth that I have built. The stories are the stones.

Kathy A. Bradley lives and writes in Bulloch County, Georgia. She is the author of *Breathing and Walking Around: Meditations on a Life*, which received the Will D. Campbell Award for Creative Nonfiction in 2010 and for which she was named 2012 Georgia Author of the Year. She is an alumna of Wesleyan College and the Walter F. George School of Law of Mercer University. Bradley currently serves as an assistant district attorney for the Ogeechee Judicial Circuit. Learn more about her at www.kathyabradley.com. *(Photo by Lori Grice.)*